Alexis de Tocqueville

A Biographical Study in Political Science

HARPER TORCHBOOKS / The Cloister Library

(Continued on next page)

HARPER TORCHBOOKS / The Academy Library

HARPER TORCHBOOKS / The Science Library

ALEXIS DE TOCQUEVILLE

Chasseriau

Alexis de Tocqueville

A Biographical Study in Political Science

J. P. MAYER

with a new essay, "Tocqueville after a Century"

HARPER TORCHBOOKS / The Academy Library
HARPER & BROTHERS
PUBLISHERS • NEW YORK

For
R. H. TAWNEY
with affection and gratitude

CONTENTS

PREFACE TO THE TORCHBOOK EDITION

During April of this year, on the occasion of the centenary of Alexis de Tocqueville's death, I took part in a colloquy in America in which nearly all American Tocqueville scholars participated. It was a fruitful and happy meeting. When, during our deliberations, America's most eminent Burke specialist referred to the present book as if no other authoritative general work on Tocqueville existed, I felt encouraged to republish it, for the English and American editions have been out of print for many years.

I felt, however, that I should not touch the basic structure of the book, though I have worked it over thoroughly. Certain allusions to events and social trends in 1939 and their interpretations I have deliberately left unchanged, even where I hold different views and would offer different interpretations now. My revision has profited from a French edition of these pages, published in 1948, and from a German edition, published in 1954; both of which were revised.

In order to facilitate the printing of this book, I have retained the references to Beaumont's edition, though my own edition, generously supported by the Rockefeller Foundation and a French State Commission, has in the meantime reached eight volumes. For Chapter Three, I refer the reader to my English and American edition of Tocqueville's *Journeys to England and Ireland* (Faber, London, and Yale University Press, New Haven); Chapter Four should perhaps be implemented by a study of Tocqueville's *Journey to America* (brought out by the same publishers). My edition of Tocqueville's *Recollections,* originally published by the Columbia University Press, is now available as a Meridian book. The editorial material which these volumes con-

tain may help the reader to widen the horizon of this provisional
sketch of Alexis de Tocqueville's life and work.

J. P. MAYER

London
December, 1959

FOREWORD

In 1925, when Antoine Redier published his pioneering work, *Comme Disait M. de Tocqueville,* he dedicated it, with justifiable irony, to "all who have been hitherto unaware of de Tocqueville."

Fourteen years have since passed, but knowledge of the great work done by de Tocqueville has increased very little in that time. Even the Library of the British Museum and the British Library for Political and Economic Science have not added Redier's book to their collections. Any new interpretation of de Tocqueville must, therefore, put before the reader the material on which it is based, even though this may detract somewhat from the smoothness of the presentation.

My thanks are due to Mr. Christopher Dawson, who has read this book in manuscript, and with whom I have been able fully to discuss important problems arising from my investigations. He is in agreement on all essential points with the conclusions I have reached. I hope that this great Catholic cultural historian will recognize my profound respect for himself and for his work, even though there are points where I have felt bound to differ from his views.

Acknowledgments are also due to Professor Lasswell and to Messrs. McGraw-Hill, London and New York, for the extract on pages 137-38

The manuscript of this book went to press a few days before Hitler began *his* war. Having written it in 1939, I saw no reason to alter a single line in the proofs. I hope that these pages may contribute to a clarification of the very essentials of the ideals and ultimate aims of our Western civilization for which we all have to fight now. Perhaps the example of Alexis de Tocqueville's life

and work as described here may nourish the hope that this fight
will not be in vain.

J. P. M.

London
September 17, 1939

INTRODUCTION

The time is ripe for a new interpretation of de Tocqueville.* In any such enterprise, however, account must be taken of the fact that de Tocqueville's writings and letters are available only in an unreliable, and indeed in part mutilated, edition issued by Gustave de Beaumont in the sixties of the last century. The family archives of the Counts de Tocqueville still contain unexplored treasures, some of which are shortly to be published by the author.

To Antoine Redier belongs the abiding honor of having discovered the true stature of de Tocqueville as a man. His book, *Comme Disait M. de Tocqueville,* is the first and has hitherto remained the only biographical analysis of one of the greatest Europeans of the nineteenth century. The following pages are deeply indebted to Redier, whose untiring and penetrating researches extending over many years have alone made a new appreciation of de Tocqueville possible.

It is noteworthy that Wilhelm Dilthey, in his *Collected Works* (vol. vii, pp. 104 et seq., Berlin, 1927), refers to the importance of Alexis de Tocqueville. "Third among the original historical thinkers of Ranke's time," he writes, "stands de Tocqueville. He is the analyst among the historical research workers of that day, *undoubtedly the most illustrious* of all political analysts since Aristotle and Machiavelli. [The italics are ours.] While Ranke and his school sorted the archives in order to come to an understanding of the network of diplomatic activity covering all Europe in recent times, these same archives served de Tocqueville for another purpose. He read them for what they could reveal of the

* I have retained on these pages the Anglo-American usage to speak of "de Tocqueville," although it would be more correct to write "Tocqueville."

abiding inner structure of the nations. He sought to analyze the interaction of functions in the modern body-politic, and preparatory to studying this intimate and enduring structural relationship he investigated political material surviving in literature, in the archives, and in life itself, with the care and nicety of a dissecting anatomist. It was he who produced the first genuine analysis of American democracy. Knowledge of the evolution of society in many lands led him to believe that here was the 'movement,' the 'continuous irresistible tendency' destined to evoke a new social order in all states. Occurrences in all parts of the world have since confirmed his judgment. A trustworthy historical and political thinker, he views this social trend of mankind neither as an advance nor as in all respects detrimental. The art of politics is bound to take this social tendency into account, and in each country to seek to harmonize the political order with it. In another of his books [Dilthey refers here to *The Ancien Régime and the Revolution*] de Tocqueville is the first to penetrate the true relation between the French political order of the eighteenth century and that of the Revolution. Political learning of this quality authorized its application in political practice. Particularly fruitful is his development of the Aristotelian dictum that a healthy constitution in any state depends on a correct relation between duties and rights, and must find some resolution of this relation which prevents rights from degenerating into privileges. Another important example of the application of his analysis in the practical field lies in his recognition of the dangers of an exaggerated centralization, and in his insight into the blessings of self-help and self-government. Thus he gathers from history itself valuable generalizations, and, by a fresh analysis of past actualities, evolves a more fundamental relation to those of the present."

Dilthey pays the foregoing tribute to de Tocqueville in his *Studien über den Aufbau der geschichtlichen Welt in den Geisteswissenschaften,* published in 1910. His words have passed unheeded, though there can hardly have been a German thinker of the prewar period who could speak with more authority than he on the intellectual-historical origins of the Western nations.

No writer in Germany has yet undertaken an analysis of de Tocqueville's works, if we except an inadequate attempt to do so by Helmut Goering in his book, *Tocqueville und die Demokratie,* published in 1928. In England there is up to the present day no book on one who was probably the most important sociologist of the nineteenth century. French writers on de Tocqueville who make his supposed liberalism their main consideration are Eugène d'Eichthal (*Alexis de Tocqueville et la Démocratie libérale,* Paris, 1897) and Pierre Marcel (*Essai politique sur Alexis de Tocqueville,* Paris, 1910). Antoine Redier retains the honor of at least envisaging the great French political thinker as that "liberal of a new kind" which de Tocqueville described himself as representing.

Political experiences following the world war and postwar periods, more especially the formation of the so-called totalitarian states, have made a re-examination of de Tocqueville's political and social precepts doubly urgent today. Neither Aristotle nor Machiavelli, with whom Dilthey very legitimately classes de Tocqueville for analytical acumen, knew anything of the phenomenon of the modern democratic mass society. De Tocqueville, on the contrary, started with the knowledge of the modern mass state as his basic political experience. It was he who originally demonstrated the structure of the modern mass state, the inevitability, in the march of destiny, of its appearance, its possible positive formation, and the equally possible negative and degenerate form it might assume. Whole libraries have been written on the political and social doctrines of Aristotle and Machiavelli, while those of de Tocqueville have been presented in few words, and there only in inadequate and misleading fashion. (The stress in Redier's important book, as we have seen, lies on the psychological and biographical planes.)

The great prophet of the Mass Age has still to be discovered. The following pages are a first attempt at such a discovery.

ONE

Childhood and Youth

The ancestral mansion of the family of Clérel de Tocqueville stands to this day in Normandy. In Alexis de Tocqueville's lifetime it was still uncertain whether the family could indeed be traced back to the time of William, the Norman conqueror of England, but today diligent search of the records has established that a Clérel de Tocqueville did indeed fight on the victorious side at the Battle of Hastings.[1]* Alexis, who had profound respect for the English political tradition, liked to dally playfully at times with the idea that ancestors of his were actually concerned in helping to lay the foundations of the English political structure.

The family history of the Clérels de Tocqueville has been carefully explored by Antoine Redier. He notes two main traits in the family character—one a deeply rooted Catholic Christianity, the other an aristocratic pride and dignity that unbent only to equals. As early as the end of the sixteenth century a Clérel championed his oppressed fellow villagers in terms reminiscent of those used by the nobles who, in 1789, made common cause with the *Tiers État*.

Alexis's father, Hervé de Tocqueville, at the age of twenty-one married Mlle. de Rosanbo, granddaughter of Louis XVI's noble and spirited defender before the revolutionary tribunal. The marriage took place two months after the execution of the king. Later in the same year Hervé de Tocqueville and his young wife were brought to Paris and there imprisoned, and only the ninth Ther-

---

* Superior numbers refer to a section of notes beginning on page 133.

1

midor saved them from the scaffold. Hervé de Tocqueville was white-haired at the age of twenty-two. His third child, Alexis, was born in Paris on July 29, 1805.

Hervé de Tocqueville entered government service under Charles X, and acted as prefect in several *départements* successively; his family did not, however, accompany him in all his wanderings. His writings reveal a mature mind and one well-schooled in history. Taine, in his *Les Origines de la France contemporaine,* vol. v. p. 390, refers in flattering terms to the Count de Tocqueville's official reports. "There is to be found in the national archives most exhaustive and accurate information concerning local government and the state of opinion among different classes of the community. . . . The letters of a number of prefects, in particular those of MM. de Chabrol and de Tocqueville, often deserved publication. Some passages in them have been marked marginally by the Minister for Home Affairs for the special attention of the King."

Alexis spent his early childhood in Verneuil, near Paris, where the family had property. His mother, it seems, never entirely recovered from the grievous experiences of the Revolution, and was always delicate and melancholic. Her heart clung to the "sweet years of her childhood when good King Louis XVI reigned" (Redier). Long after, in 1857, two years before his death, Alexis conjured up the personality of his mother as he had seen her in his early childhood: "I remember as though it were yesterday a certain evening in my father's château; a family festivity had brought us and our nearest relations together. The servants had retired. We were all sitting about the hearth. My mother, who had a sweet and touching voice, began to sing an air well known during our civil disturbances to words relating to Louis XVI and his death. When she ceased all were weeping, not for the personal sufferings they had undergone, not even for the loss of so many of our blood in the civil war and on the scaffold, but for the fate of a man who had died fifteen years earlier, and whom most of those who shed tears for him had never seen. But that man had been the King."[2]

Such was the world in which Alexis passed his early childhood.

The upbringing of the children, of whom Alexis was the youngest, two brothers having been born before him, rested with the Abbé Lesueur, who had already been charged with the education of Alexis's father, Hervé de Tocqueville. Very little is known about the abbé beyond the fact that Alexis's grandmother, a deeply pious Catholic, had chosen him as her son's preceptor. When, in 1831, Alexis learned in America of his tutor's death, he was deeply moved, and wrote to his brother Edward: "I loved our good old friend as I did our father." Certain it is that Alexis owed the uprightness of his character to the old priest, who alone taught him the Christian virtues—to do the good and eschew the evil—and his gratitude did not cease with his teacher's death. "Never again," he writes from America to his beloved brother, "shall we meet a man whose whole faculties and affections are centered upon ourselves. He seems to have lived for us alone."

During the six years of Count Hervé de Tocqueville's prefect-ship in Metz, Alexis completed his studies at the *lycée* in that town. His career at school was a brilliant one, a special prize and two first prizes being awarded to him. There were many lonely hours, too, during which the boy browsed in his father's library. At sixteen years he was reading books hardly accessible to the average boy of his age. It was at this time that he lost the religious belief to which he was to return only in the last years of his life. Among his early papers are some fragments, included by Gustave de Beaumont in the biographical notice with which he prefaces the complete edition of his friend's works, which show a young mind wrestling hard with the theories of Descartes. "There is no Absolute Truth," writes de Tocqueville in these early papers. And again: "If I were asked to classify human miseries I should rank them in the following order: (1) Disease; (2) Death; (3) Doubt."[3] Shattered for him was the strict Catholic belief of his ancestors, gone all but a Christian deism.

Alexis de Tocqueville's basic inclination for critical and original thinking seems to have been developing in these years. Sainte-Beuve truly established later that de Tocqueville had read comparatively little. His was a mind to concentrate on concrete matters, and to formulate their laws with devoted precision. He completed his studies of law at the age of twenty, and then set out with his brother Edward on an educational tour which took him to Italy and Sicily.

Gustave de Beaumont has given us some typical fragments from the voluminous journals kept by Alexis de Tocqueville during this journey, and these, for all their youthful character, foretell the methods of the mature man. There is, for instance, an account of the social structure of landed property in a part of Sicily. From the facts he proceeds to an explanation of causes, and from the causal analysis he educes the norm of appropriate political action. "Whence," asks the young thinker, "comes this extreme parcelling out of land, which in France is regarded by many intelligent people as an evil? Are we to consider it as advantageous or the reverse for Sicily? The explanation is not difficult. I note the fact that in an enlightened country, where the climate conduces to activity, and where all classes wish (as in England, for example) to grow rich, nothing but harm can come to agriculture and hence to the domestic prosperity of the country concerned, from the exaggerated parcelling-out of land, since this method stands in the way of great possibilities of improving the soil, and of the effectiveness of those persons who have the will and the capacity to exploit such possibilities. But when the opposite is the case, and it is a question of awakening and stimulating a miserable and half-paralysed people for whom passivity is a pleasure, and whose upper classes are dulled by vices or inherited indolence, I can think of no more welcome expedient than this parcelling-out of land. Were I king of England I would favour large estates; were I lord of Sicily I would vigorously support small holdings; but as I am neither I return with all speed to my diary."[4] The typical habit of mind of the twenty-two-year-old writer, his exact eye for detail, his analytical dissection, and his abstraction of the structural political law underlying the details are unmistakable in this passage. Clear, too, is the political application, although it is presented in somewhat frolicsome manner. De Tocqueville is, however, still far from an original comprehensive view of the whole social body-politic. With youthful uncriticalness he adopts the climatic theories of Bodin and to some extent also of Montesquieu, whose great works were doubtless familiar to him. Later he definitely rejected the fatalistic naturalism of the climatic dogma and its associated race theory. On this he was later to write on the last page of his book on America: "I know that several of my contemporaries have thought that the peoples of the earth are never their own masters, and that they must of necessity obey I know not what dark and unconquerable forces generated from early experiences of the race, from the soil, and from the climate. These are false and cowardly doctrines, which can produce only weak individuals and faint-hearted nations. Providence has created man neither wholly independent nor wholly enslaved. Doubtless each man has his own circle of destiny from which he cannot escape, but within its wide circumference he is powerful and free; and the same is true of nations."[5] In these sentences speaks the mature mind of the thirty-five-year-old thinker, and they reveal how significant was de Tocqueville's development during the intervening thirteen years.

There is another passage in these sketches which should also, perhaps, be rescued from oblivion. Alexis is suddenly filled with an intense longing for home, for France. Perhaps it is only in a foreign land that one can appreciate the real worth of one's native land. He writes: "On foreign soil all things are tinged with sadness, often even pleasure itself."[6] Not until one is far away do things which have become overfamiliarized by custom attain their true stature and appear in their authentic colors. The young de Tocqueville was no traveler for travel's sake. He missed France, *his* France, while he experienced foreign institutions. When later he set himself to obtain full knowledge of the institutions and structures of democratic America, his sole purpose was to understand the structure of his own country, then undergoing profound changes. Thus his last book, as will be seen, has for theme the French social structure, which he studies in transition from the

Ancien régime to Revolution, his true purpose being to act as retrospective interpreter of these events.

The two young men were not entirely satisfied with the journey, for the results arrived at were not proportionate with the time and toil expended. "The harvest, it is true, was not commensurate with the effort, so that, as far as we are concerned, there was a waste of energy and enterprise. But even if the end was futile, still we pursued it as if it had value, and we achieved it. My present concern—and so I close this diary—is to pray God for one favour—that He may one day grant me to desire with equal intensity some matter that *is* worth the pains."[7] Four years later Alexis, with his friend Gustave de Beaumont, set out upon his journey to America, a journey which was to provide a testimony of divine favor on so disciplined, almost puritanical, an ambition.

Alexis was appointed, by royal patent, to a judgeship in the law courts of Versailles, where his father had already been in residence for a year as prefect of the *département* of Seine-et-Oise.

TWO

Calling and Vocation

The young magistrate concentrated on his work. He was sometimes afraid lest he should become a mere routine man and copyist like many of his colleagues, yet he would prefer, as he wrote to an intimate friend, to burn all his books than to grow "incapable of judging a great movement or of guiding a great undertaking."[1]

The July revolution of 1830 was no surprise to de Tocqueville. It implied the final victory of bourgeois France. In the *Souvenirs* (a broad survey of his life as a politician, which he undertook as a kind of *apologia* in July 1850 after his resignation from his post as minister for foreign affairs and which was not published until long after his death) he explains the critical significance of the July revolution in the social history of France. Although this account dates from twenty years later, and carries the weight of those twenty years' riper political judgment behind it, it requires mention here since the great political thinker's basic views on this matter were already established in 1830. "Our history from 1789 to 1830, viewed at a distance and as a whole, affords the spectacle of an embittered struggle between the *ancien régime* with its traditions, its memories, its hopes, and its personnel, represented by the aristocracy, and the new France under the leadership of the middle class. The year 1830 closed this first period of our revolutions—or rather of our revolution, for there is but *one* revolution, the same under all the changes of fortune, of which our fathers saw the beginning, and of which we ourselves in all probability shall not see the end. In 1830 the triumph of the middle class was definitive, and so complete that all political powers, franchises, prerogatives, the government in its entirety, came to be confined and as it were accumulated within the narrow limits of this one class to the exclusion of all below it, and indeed of all above it. . . . The spirit peculiar to the middle class became the general spirit of the Government, dominating foreign as well as home affairs—a bustling, industrious spirit, often dishonest, orderly for the most part, sometimes courageous through vanity and egotism, temperamentally timid, moderate in all things except in the desire for easy living and mediocrity—a spirit which mingled with that of the people or of the aristocracy can work wonders, but which in isolation can only produce a Government without virtue or greatness."[2]

This passage not only contains de Tocqueville's axiomatic concepts of the health of the body politic, but furthermore makes plain why, as a politician, he absolutely repudiated the bourgeois monarchy of Louis Philippe. He did not, however, quit the service, but succeeded (the more easily, perhaps, as son of the Prefect for Seine-et-Oise) in obtaining from the new minister of the interior leave to pursue an investigation of the penal system of the United States of America.

To take the oath to the new king occasioned him the deepest distress, even though he condemned the Bourbons as cowards "who deserve not one-thousandth part of the blood that has been shed in their cause." It is worth while in these days of conscienceless shifting from one regime to another to consider the profound conscientiousness, the lofty and honorable moral standard shown by this young Frenchman. "I have just taken the oath! My conscience reproaches me not at all, but I suffer none the less profoundly for that, and I shall count this day as one of the unhappiest of my life. For the first time since my birth I have to avoid the presence of persons whom I esteem even while I disapprove of them. Oh Marie, the idea of it racks me! All the pride in me revolts; and yet I have not failed in my duty! I have done what I owe to my country, whose only salvation lies in a rule which has arisen to save us from anarchy. But have I done all I owe to myself, to my family, to those who died for the cause I have ceased to serve when all are forsaking it? I am not a child. I have no idea of abandoning myself to feeble regrets. But I feel keenly enough the wound I have just received. I feel it more than I can say. I am at war with myself. That is a new state of things to me, and a terrible one. I have taken the first step. Where will it lead me? Oh, how right I was to speak of civil war! How simple the path would have been if duty had accorded with all the susceptibilities of honour. . . . How my voice changed as I uttered those three words! I felt my heart beat as though it would burst from my breast."[3]

When almost twenty years later de Tocqueville had to swear another oath, this time to the Prince-President Louis Napoleon, he was, no doubt, moved by similar feelings.

In April 1831 Alexis de Tocqueville and his friend and colleague Gustave de Beaumont embarked for New York. Their mission was frankly no more than a pretext to de Tocqueville, whose real intention was to study at first hand the only completely democratic state and society of his time. All the same he did not shirk his obligation to study the American penal system. The results of the numerous observations made in the United States by these two young French magistrates, with the ready and friendly aid of their American hosts, were embodied in a book published in 1833 under both their names, and entitled *The American Penal System and Its Application in France*. Here is not the place to consider in detail de Tocqueville's first book. It shows thorough acquaintance with its subject, and a most careful working-out of statistical detail. The French authorities were satisfied, and de Tocqueville himself gained a reputation as an expert on the prison system.

The American journey occupied ten months, and carried the two friends through many states of the union, even as far as the then primeval forest regions on the shores of Lake Michigan. De Tocqueville wanted actually to see those as yet unoccupied regions of northeastern America whose civilization still lay in the future. A fortnight's hard and rough travel on horseback brought them to Saginaw Bay. De Tocqueville describes this ride through the American wilderness in pages published posthumously under the title *A Fortnight in the Wilderness,* wherein he shows a keenness of observation reminiscent of Alexander von Humboldt's travel papers. The hardships faced by the two travelers often involved real danger to life and limb. On one occasion when their steamer went aground de Tocqueville caught a very severe chill which may have resulted in that weakening of the lungs which led to his premature death.

The friends returned to France in 1832, and at once fulfilled their official contract by writing their *Penal System.* They had unexpected leisure for the work, for Gustave de Beaumont resigned his legal post on account of the conduct of a high official which he regarded as "dishonorable," while Alexis ranged himself beside his friend and petitioned his superiors for immediate discharge. "Long united in intimate friendship with the person who has just been dismissed from his functions, whose opinions I hold, and whose conduct I approve, I think myself bound voluntarily to share his lot, and to abandon with him a career in which neither active service nor upright conduct is a security against unmerited disgrace."[4]

With these estimable sentiments Alexis de Tocqueville left the French judiciary service. He moved into a modest apartment in Paris, and began the work which was the real purpose of his American journey, and whose publication was to bring him world renown. At seven-and-twenty he saw his future clear. A great work lay before him; his apprentice years were over; he went forward to the harvest.

THREE

Years of Early Maturity

The two years during which Alexis de Tocqueville wrote his book *Democracy in America* were possibly the happiest of his life. He applied to this voluminous work the full intensity of his newly ripened powers. He modeled his style upon that of the great French seventeenth-century classics, but above all upon that of Pascal, who among the masters of French literature was perhaps his spiritual next-of-kin. "These two minds," wrote de Beaumont, "were made for one another." It was not alone the penetrating logic of Pascal's style which deeply influenced de Tocqueville, for he had that in the depths of his soul which responded to the Jansenistical rigorism of Pascal's morality.

De Tocqueville also read at this time with a tireless appetite (de Beaumont is again our authority) the works of Plato, Plutarch, Machiavelli, Rousseau, and Montesquieu, and it would seem that in these same years he made a close study of Aristotle, Polybius, and, more particularly, the works of Edmund Burke. He felt a need to measure the wealth of his American observations against the whole Western heritage of political doctrine.

During these two years he interrupted his work only once when in 1833 he went to England, but this was an interruption of a special kind. He clearly felt that he could not finish his book on America without personal study of the peculiar characteristics of the English state. Actually the American book was not designed as a mere interpretive description of the American state. De Tocqueville had long since concluded that there had been a process of increasing democratization of the Western states since the eleventh century, and he wanted to formulate the essential structures of this general social evolutionary tendency. A study of the kind would today be called a sociological study, and de Tocqueville is, in fact, one of the greatest masters of sociology, a contemporary of Auguste Comte, who was the first to mark out the particular sphere of this science. Notes made by de Tocqueville for his own information during his first English journey of about a month's duration are naturally contributory to his great theme. An entry under the date of September 7, 1833,[1] shows him in search of a kind of common denominator for the whole. He reached England in the expectation of finding that country on the eve of violent revolutionary events. The electoral Reform Bill had just been passed, and the aristocratic principle upon which, in his opinion, the English social order had rested hitherto was daily losing ground; would the democratic principle take its place? Yet de Tocqueville doubted whether this change would be accomplished *by force*. He saw clearly that the English aristocracy was quite unlike any of the continental nobilities. It was accessible to all, and therefore hard to define, while, furthermore, the entire social order rested upon an aristocratic pedestal. No doubt there was overt hostility to the nobility, but public opinion, as it seemed to de Tocqueville, was far from wishing to sweep away the nobility in cold blood. He found traces of aristocratic rights of succession even among the middle classes, and perhaps he should also have noted the rich bourgeoisie's chances of social advancement which provided the English nobility with a bulwark against the spearhead of revolutionary onslaught.

De Tocqueville did not overlook the wretched condition of the English proletariat, but even the unjust distribution of land in the great landed estates, which were in the hands of a comparative minority, gave no ground to expect an agrarian revolutionary movement. The average Englishman regarded this condition of things as necessary for the economic well-being of the country as a whole. To the sociologist, therefore, it seemed probable that the English would succeed in modifying their political and social condition by natural evolution, without civil war or commotion. De Tocqueville's prophecy in this matter has held good to the present day. Even now the place of the English nobility in England's social fabric is unshaken. The very language points to the difference between the English and the French nobilities. The concept of the *gentleman* constitutes a *universal* social norm, valid for *all* classes of the English social body; The French *gentilhomme,* on the contrary, carries the idea of a caste barrier, and applies exclusively to the nobility. Because of its privileged status the French nobility inevitably evoked a reaction of hate among the bourgeois (and later among the proletarian) classes which is, in fact, unknown in the English social consciousness even to the present day. During centuries of evolution the English aristocracy has actually become a *functional* nobility, whereas the continental nobilities for the most part cut themselves off from the pulsing life of their nations and were, relatively speaking, shut out from it.

The specialized political function of the English aristocracy was certainly one of the determining factors in de Tocqueville's deep veneration for England. In the course of his very thorough researches into de Tocqueville's unpublished papers Antoine Redier came upon a document which has a bearing on this point, reminding one by its positively Pascalian honesty of the famous *Mémorial,*[2] and showing very distinctly de Tocqueville's instinctive adherence to the aristocracy. The confession reads as follows:

My Instinct, My Opinions

Experience has taught me that almost all men (and most certainly I myself) return always more or less to certain fundamental instincts, and only do well what conforms with these instincts. Let me try sincerely to discover where lie my *fundamental instincts* and where my *true principles.*

Intellectually I have an inclination for democratic institutions, but I am an aristocrat by instinct—that is to say, I despise and fear the mass.

I have a passionate love for liberty, law, and respect for rights— but not for democracy. There is the ultimate truth of my heart! I am neither of the revolutionary party nor of the conservative. Nevertheless, when all is said, I hold more by the latter than the former. For I differ from the latter more as to means than as to end, while I differ from the former both as to means and end.

Liberty is my foremost passion. This is the truth![3]

Though this *Mémorial* is perhaps of a later date, it nonetheless outlines very sharply its author's basic social-philosophical attitude.

It is significant that the notes on the English journey of 1833 close with the following passage: "Here (in England) freedom is not a Right of Man but a special privilege of the Englishman. (The German, for his part, will tell you that it is a fruit of education.)"[4]

De Tocqueville found the norm of his ideal state in the structure of the English state. So far, in dealing with the English notes, we have touched only on the sociological principles therein displayed, and it is desirable to come rather nearer to the concrete, even though we do not intend to attempt to reproduce the entire content of these notes. Two points, however, may be mentioned here. De Tocqueville refers to a conversation he had with an Englishman about the decentralization of government in England. "England," he reports the Englishman as saying, "is the land of decentralization. We have a central government, but not a central administration. Each county, each borough, each district looks after its own interests. Industry is left to itself. . . . It is not in the nature of things that a central government should be able to supervise all the wants of a great nation. Decentralization is the chief cause of England's material progress."[5]

Next day de Tocqueville adds the following commentary: "Most of those people in France who speak against centralization do not really wish to see it abolished; some because they hold power, others because they expect to hold it. It is with them as it was with the pretorians, who voluntarily suffered the tyranny of the emperor because each of them might one day become emperor. . . . Decentralization, like liberty, is a thing which leaders promise their people, but which they never give them. To get it and to keep it the people must count on their own sole efforts: if they do not care to do so the evil is beyond remedy."[6]

Decentralized government thus serves as a school of freedom. One of the most important conclusions of the forthcoming book on America was already established in this passage.

De Tocqueville was greatly concerned to observe that the Anglican Church, the established church, was losing prestige, and he compares her situation with that of the Catholic Church in France before 1789. He found, however, three grounds for supposing that a less dismal fate might await the Anglican Church. Firstly, numerous sects were winning the esteem that the established church was forfeiting; secondly, he held that the English had less passion and less imagination than the French, and might be the better able to distinguish between the Church and its ministers; thirdly, he thought the English people more earnest than the French—and earnest characters are more disposed to religious ideas. Here again the French thinker discerned an element essential in the English national character and one which has shown no change up to the present day.

A splendid fragment of writing comparing the English Puritan revolution of 1640 with the French revolution of 1789 closes the notes on this first English journey. Both revolutions were entered upon in the name of freedom and equality, but the English revolution was carried through under the badge of *Freedom,* whereas the French movement bore *Equality* inscribed upon its banners.[7] It is apparent here how deeply de Tocqueville pursued his analysis of the sociological substance of the two nations. Experience of England brought de Tocqueville's historical judgment to ripening point, and nothing now stood in the way of the completion of his book on America.

Letters of introduction opened doors for de Tocqueville in London, and in this way he at once made the acquaintance of Nassau William Senior, an economist of weight and influence, with whom he formed a lifelong friendship. Senior kept records of his correspondence with de Tocqueville and of conversations with him. They were published in 1872 under the title *Corre-*

spondence and Conversations of Alexis de Tocqueville with Nassau William Senior—a notable memorial to a fruitful friendship, and to posterity an important supplement to Gustave de Beaumont's edition of letters, writings, and speeches.*

There is, however, yet another explanation of de Tocqueville's rapid penetration of the English world, for nothing helped him so much toward an understanding of a foreign land as the assimilation of his spirit to it through the mediumship of a beloved woman. Since 1828 Alexis de Tocqueville had been in love with Mary Mottley, an English lady who, living under her aunt's roof, was his near neighbor in Versailles. Mary Mottley was nine years older than he, but he found in her nonetheless his true companion for life. We have already quoted a passage from a letter which suggests how absolute were the confidence and understanding between these two. Although de Tocqueville's family appear to have energetically opposed their union, de Tocqueville's own wishes eventually prevailed with them, and the marriage took place on October 26, 1836.

Mary Mottley possessed neither great beauty nor a fortune—the two grounds held sufficient for matrimony by average opinion in France. But de Tocqueville was not to be measured by any average, and in this woman he must have found the human support necessary for his otherwise lonely career. It is true that his life brought him success and renown in plenty, but to the last he felt himself alone and misunderstood in regard to his real goal. He found the ordinary social round boring and empty, but kept in close touch with a handful of friends who remained true to him to his life's end. His parliamentary activities necessarily brought him contacts with many people, but here, too, as he says in his *Souvenirs,* he was unable to "make a general habit of frequenting people, since I never know more than a very few. When a man does not strike me by something rare in his intellect or his sentiments it is as if I did not see him. I have always supposed that mediocre men possess nose, mouth, and eyes just as men of merit,

* A new and more complete edition of these papers will be published as part of my edition of the *Œuvres complètes.*

but I have never been able to fix in my memory the peculiar shape of these features in any one of them. I am always asking the names of these strangers whom I see every day, and I always forget them. I do not despise them, but I have little to do with them, and I treat them as commonplaces."[8] De Tocqueville's special intellectual quality shows itself even in the way his visual memory works. He gave affecting expression to his sense of isolation in a letter to Mme. Swetchine, a close friend of his later years: "My contemporaries and I go by more and more divergent ways—sometimes such *opposite* ways, that we can hardly ever now meet with like feelings and like thoughts. . . . I have relations, neighbours, people who are close to me; but my mind has neither family nor motherland. I assure you, my dear Madam, that such spiritual and moral isolation often gives me a sense of loneliness more intense than any I ever experienced in the primeval forests of America."[9]

De Tocqueville's recollection of his own sense of terror at the boundless loneliness of the primeval forests of America justifies the quotation here of this letter of much later date, for few men have been so conscious in early manhood of their own dispositions and their own life's tasks.

De Tocqueville might not, like Pascal, wrestle with his God in solitude. He tried to find God in the things of the world. The world and its many-sided experiences were for him a necessary if roundabout way, but one that nonetheless led at last to the goal. A letter written from Berne on July 24, 1836, to Eugène Stoffels, a boyhood friend, gives a clear indication of the fundamentally religious trend of his political philosophy. "You seem to me to have understood the general ideas on which my programme rests. What most and *always* [the italics are ours] amazes me about my country, more especially these last few years, is to see ranged on the one side men who value morality, religion and order, and upon the other those who love liberty and the equality of men before the law. This strikes me as the most extraordinary and deplorable spectacle ever offered to the eyes of man; for all the things thus separated are, I am certain, indissolubly united in the sight of God. They are all *holy* things, if I may so express myself, because the greatness and the happiness of man in this world can only result from their union. It seems to me, therefore, that one of the finest enterprises of our time would be to demonstrate that these things are not incompatible; that, on the contrary, they are bound up together in such a fashion that each of them is weakened by separation from the rest. Such is my basic idea."[10] I believe that the human state-order, in its essence and totality, has found no such exemplary formulation as this since the writings of Aristotle. It is true that Thomas Aquinas in his *De regimine principum* restated the Aristotelian political philosophy in accordance with the medieval ordering of temporal and spiritual life, but this medieval hierarchic order had since dissolved beyond recall. Machiavelli, Bodin, Hobbes, Rousseau, and Montesquieu had attempted to interpret man as *zoon politikon* from a consideration of his natural activities, but de Tocqueville was the first to attempt once more to display the natural and creaturely ordering of mankind in its single indissoluble actuality. No one since then has followed him on this road.

In the above-quoted letter to Stoffels there is a passage about the book *Democracy in America:* "I have shown, and shall continue to show, a lively and rational passion for liberty, and this for two reasons. In the first place it is my profound conviction, and in the second I do not wish to be identified with those lovers of order who are ready to sell free will and our laws cheap for the sake of sleeping safely in their beds. There are enough of them already, and I dare to prophesy that they will never achieve anything great or durable. I shall show my taste for liberty frankly, then, and a general desire to see it developed in all the political institutions of my country. But at the same time I shall profess so great a respect for justice, so true a love for order and law, so deep and so reasonable an attachment for morality and religious beliefs, that I cannot but believe people will see plainly in me a *liberal of a new kind* [the italics are ours] and will not confuse me with the majority of the democrats of our day."[11] The passage stresses the fact that the writer is not one of those who can sail with any breeze. It was the more needful for such a man to have a life companion of a special kind. Mary Mottley intimately revealed England to de Tocqueville. His letters to her, of which Antoine Redier gives us some examples, show between the pair an uncommonly close union whose fulcrum is to be sought perhaps rather in the realm of comradeship and ethics than in that of the actually erotic. "I swear to you, my dearest," he wrote to her, "that I believe my love for you makes me a better man. When I think of you I feel that my soul is exalted."[12]

In Mary he found inexhaustible sources of tenderness and patience. Even her perhaps typically English liking for pet dogs, who were treated almost like children (there were none of the marriage), did nothing to injure the love of her sensitive French husband. She was often unbearably capricious, yet his kindness was unfailing. It is not easy to fathom the soul of an English-woman. She is little given to emotional expression, and can only be judged in action. Fortunately there is a passage in a letter to Mme. Swetchine which plainly shows the hidden role of Mary Mottley in de Tocqueville's life. He writes on February 11, 1857:

"I have always been subject to a vague restlessness, and a longing for I know not what. Though this malady has become chronic, I wonder that I suffer from it so much under circum-stances in which I ought to enjoy peace. Assuredly I cannot com-plain, and I do not wish to complain, of the lot which Providence has assigned to me. Still, the most essential of the conditions of happiness fails me, the power of quietly enjoying the present. Yet I have by my side a person whose society ought long ago to have cured me of this great, though absurd misery. And in fact, this society has been most salutary to me. For the last twenty years it has kept my mind from giving way, but has not rendered it per-fectly and habitually steady. My wife, whom the world little knows, thinks and feels strongly. Misfortune affects her sharply and violently, but she can thoroughly enjoy happiness. She does not waste herself in vain agitation. She floats calmly and quietly down the current of tranquil days and favourable circumstances. The serenity of our home sometimes extends to me, but I soon lose it, and relapse into the idle useless excitement in which my mind keeps turning like a wheel out of gear."[13] In the company of such a personality a man may experience a placidity which is not part of his own nature. Perhaps Englishwomen are specially endowed with this placid quality. De Tocqueville was a master in the portrayal and understanding of people, and he knew his wife's character through and through.

He was five-and-twenty years old when he first came under the spell of this Puritan lady nine years his senior. It is not infrequently the destiny of men who mature early—and de Tocqueville matured remarkably early—to find in women older than themselves that intuitive command of life which their own experience has not and could not yet have taught them.

FOUR

Democracy in America

The first two volumes of de Tocqueville's work on America appeared in January 1835. They achieved unexampled success almost overnight, bringing to him the fame of a great European author. "Nothing like it," declared Royer-Collard, "has appeared since Montesquieu." In the Parisian salons such men as Chateaubriand and Lamartine treated the young political philosopher with great deference. In England a long review of the work, written by the intellectual leader of English radicalism, John Stuart Mill, appeared in the *London and Westminster Review,* and a German translation was instantly to follow. In America, too, the work of the Frenchman was immediately recognized as a classical interpretation of American political conditions, a pre-eminence it retains today as one of the most read textbooks on American constitutional life.

In May, de Tocqueville, with Gustave de Beaumont, made his second journey to England. His reception from this time onward was everywhere a brilliant one. Letters of introduction were no longer necessary—his book opened every door to him. He was asked by a committee of members of the House of Commons for his expert opinion on the question of suffrage guarantees, his report being some months later the subject of a notice by Sir Robert Peel. Great things had been accomplished, his earlier aspirations realized.

Before attempting to summarize the principal contents of the work on America we may quote a letter which de Tocqueville wrote while in the United States to de Chabrol—his first from American soil, and of major importance because it already contains in essence the conclusions of *Democracy in America*. This letter, which remained unpublished until 1925, is among Antoine Redier's many happy finds.

"Picture to yourself, my dear friend, if you can, a society which comprises all the nations of the world—English, French, German: people differing from one another in language, in beliefs, in opinions; in a word a society possessing no roots, no memories, no prejudices, no routine, no common ideas, no national character, yet with a happiness a hundred times greater than our own. More virtuous? I doubt it. This, then, is our starting point! What is the connecting link between these so different elements? How are they welded into one people? *By community of interests.* That is the secret! Personal interest is a continual factor, declares itself openly, and even asserts itself as a social theory. In this matter, it must be admitted, we are very far from the ancient republics, yet this nation is republican, and I do not doubt will remain so for some considerable length of time. And the best form of government for it is a republic. I can only explain this phenomenon on reflection that present-day America is so happily placed in a physical sense that private interest is never contrary to public interest, which is certainly not the case in Europe.

"What are the general influences which induce men to undertake nefarious practices against the State? On the one hand the desire for power, on the other the difficulties of creating for themselves a happy existence by ordinary means. Here there is no public authority, and to tell the truth there is no need for one. The States have few soldiers, because they have no enemies, and consequently no armies; there is neither taxation nor central government. Executive power, being non-existent, is a source neither of money nor of power.* So long as things remain as they

---

* On this point de Tocqueville had later to revise his first impressions to a considerable extent. By the time he reached the third volume of his work on America he had achieved a more adequate appreciation of the preponderance of the executive function over that of all other political spheres within the modern mass state.

are, where is the need for fretting ambition? In examining the other side of this state of affairs the same conclusion is arrived at, for, if politics afford little scope, there remain a thousand other careers open to human activity.

"The whole world over here seems to consist of malleable matter which man forms and fashions to his liking. An immense field, for the most part undeveloped, lies open to industry. There is no man who cannot reasonably expect to attain the amenities of life, for each knows that, given love of work, his future is certain. Thus, in this happy land, there is nothing to draw the restless spirit of man towards political passions. All, on the contrary, tends to direct him to an activity which has no dangers for the State. I would that all those who dream, in the name of America, of a republic for France, could come and see it here in the working!

"The last reason which I have just given you is, in my judgment, the principal explanation of the two dominant characteristics which distinguish this nation, namely, its industrial genius and the variability of its character. Nothing is easier in America than to acquire wealth; it is natural, therefore, that the human mind, which demands a ruling passion, ends by fastening all its thoughts on gain. The result of this is that at first sight the people here seem to be a nation of merchants met together to trade, and that in proportion as one obtains deeper insight into the American character one sees the more clearly that one question alone decides the value of everything in this world—how much money will it bring in?

"As for inconstancy of character it is apparent in a thousand ways. An American takes up ten occupations in a lifetime, leaving them and returning to them again: he continually changes his place of abode, and perpetually undertakes new enterprises. Less than any man does he fear to jeopardize the fortune he has acquired, for he knows with what ease he can found a new one.

"Besides, change seems to him the natural state of man, and how should it be otherwise? Everything around him keeps up an incessant movement—law and opinions, public officials, fortunes, even the earth herself changes her face from day to day. Surrounded by this universal movement it would be impossible for the American to remain passive. Thus one must not seek here for that family spirit nor for those venerable traditions of honour and of virtue which so eminently distinguish several of our old European countries. A people which appears to live only to get rich can hardly be, in the strict acceptation of the word, virtuous; but it is a steady people. There are none of the fripperies which belong to idle luxury; people's habits are regular; there is little or no time to give to women, who seem here to count only as mothers of families and mistresses of homes. What is incontestable is that morals are pure. The *roué* of Europe is absolutely unknown in America; the passion for money-making leads and dominates all other passions.

"You will realize, my dear friend, that these are only impressions—I have been here so short a time."[1]

In these sentences de Tocqueville summarizes his first, strongly intuitive impression of America, an impression which was destined later to be set down in exact manner in the first two volumes of his work on America. It is not intended here to give an exhaustive analysis of the line of thought pursued by de Tocqueville in his *Democracy in America,* allusion to some of the major points contained therein being sufficient, especially as John Stuart Mill, in the second volume of his *Dissertations and Discussions,* and James Bryce, in his *Studies in History and in Jurisprudence,* have both provided excellent analyses of this work. There is, too, d'Eichthal's study (included in the book to which earlier reference has been made), which may still be read with profit. All the same, it is almost disgraceful that there should be, in view of the importance of de Tocqueville's work, so scanty a harvest of critical and useful literature regarding it. One could wish that even a small portion of the mass of commentary on, for instance, Aristotle's *Politics* or on Montesquieu's *L'Esprit des lois,* could have been devoted to the great work of the French thinker.[1a]

In the first two volumes of the work on America (following the arrangement of the first edition) de Tocqueville begins by examining the share taken by the Anglo-Saxon part of the population in building up the United States in America. From this point he proceeds to an analysis of the separate states in that union, which analysis he believed necessary to a comprehension of the importance and of the functions of the central government. Before, however, describing, in Chapter VIII of the first volume, the federal union, de Tocqueville gives a suggestive explanation of the American legal system.

The second volume opens with an account of American party organization, which is followed by an investigation into the state of public opinion and the function of political associations in the United States; de Tocqueville then proceeds with his analysis of the problems that government of democracy in America raises. Chapters VI and VII are of particular importance, for in them de Tocqueville examines the "tyranny of democratic majorities" and the possibilities of mitigating the dangers arising therefrom. In the last chapter but one (Chapter IX of the second volume) an enumeration is undertaken of the grounds which seem to de Tocqueville to guarantee for the future the duration of a democratic republic in the United States; while the last chapter deals with the different races of mankind inhabiting the country, with a final series of cautious conjectures on the probable future condition of these races.

Thus may be summarized the general trend of de Tocqueville's researches. What are their most important conclusions? For centuries the Western world has been moving in the direction of social freedom and equality. De Tocqueville had been made aware, by the particular dynamic of French social development, that freedom and equality, which had been raised by the great French Revolution to be mankind's basic demands, are by no means inalienable the one from the other. Plainly the revolution of 1789, though restoring civic equality, did nothing to bring liberty to individual man. The principle in political life of equality without freedom seems to de Tocqueville to be as untenable as that of freedom without equality. How can the co-ordination of freedom with equality be assured? De Tocqueville felt the essential importance of such a co-ordination, and sought to extract the norms of it from the nature and operation of the North American political institutions: independent administration of communities, freedom of religious belief and of the press, security of judicial independence; above all, centralization of government (necessary within certain bounds) without overemphasis. At this point de Tocqueville's analysis reaches a depth which will establish for all time his place among the great masters of Western political thought. In *Democracy in America* (Chapter VII, vol. ii) he writes:

"A general law has been made and sanctioned, not only by a majority of this or that people, but by a majority of mankind. *This law bears the name of Justice.* [The italics are ours.] The rights of every people are consequently confined within the limits of what is just. A nation may be considered in the light of a jury which is empowered to represent society at large, and to apply the great and general law of Justice. Ought such a jury, which respesents society, to have more power than the society in which the laws it applies originate? When I refuse to obey an unjust law I do not contest the right which the majority has of commanding, but I simply appeal from the sovereignty of the people to the sovereignty of mankind. It has been asserted that a people can never entirely outstep the boundaries of justice and of reason in those affairs which are more peculiarly its own; and that consequently full power may fearlessly be given to the majority by which it is represented. *But this language is that of a slave.* [The italics are ours.] I am, therefore, of opinion that some one social power must always be made to predominate over the others; but I think that liberty is endangered when this power is checked by no obstacle which may retard its course and force it to moderate its own vehemence.

"Unlimited power appears to me to be in itself an evil and a dangerous thing; and the mind of man unequal to the disinterested practice of omnipotence. I think that God alone can exercise supreme and uncontrolled power, because His wisdom and justice are eternally proportionate to His might. But no power on earth is so worthy of honour for itself, or of reverential obedience to the rights which it represents, that I would consent to admit its uncontrolled and all-predominant authority. When I see that the right and the means of absolute command are conferred on a people or upon a king, upon an aristocracy or a democracy, a monarchy or a republic, I recognize the germ of tyranny, and I journey onwards to a land of more hopeful institutions.

"In my opinion the main evil of the present democratic institutions of the United States does not arise, as is often asserted in Europe, from their weakness, but from their overpowering strength; and I am not so much alarmed at the excessive liberty which reigns in that country as at the very inadequate securities which exist against tyranny."[2]

Some have considered de Tocqueville's conception of sovereignty, as he formulates it in the preceding sentences, to be, logically speaking, not conclusive enough—an objection which seems to me entirely baseless. The abatement, by means of political devices, of undivided sovereignty—political despotism as he calls it—is in no way de Tocqueville's intention. His desire is to guarantee the freedom of the individual by creating an equilibrium in the state. He conceives of the state as being subject to a higher norm, the idea of justice, against which idea the state is ever, in the last instance, to be measured. Thus the state is not in itself, as Hegel would have it, the realization of the moral idea, but possesses the capacity of attaining this ultimate moral norm only in a supreme instance, namely, by nonviolation of the idea of justice. For de Tocqueville actuality and idea of the state constitute a tension. The state is interpreted by him as an approximation to the "Norm of Justice." De Tocqueville had not read his Plato in vain. It appears then as if this elemental factor in the conceptions of the great Frenchman has hitherto received insufficient attention. James Bryce, in an appreciation of de Tocqueville's method, which he published before writing his own *American Commonwealth,* remarks that the facts cited by the former are rather the illustrations of conclusions than their sources. Bryce was, however, far from perceiving that the *real*

presuppositions of de Tocqueville's way of thinking lie in the
realm of political philosophy, and are there alone to be sought.

De Tocqueville cherished a profound belief in the essential
freedom and equality of man, and held that only under a political
regime which succeeded in establishing these two indispensable
conditions could the dignity of man be inviolably assured. These
presuppositions alone make possible any understanding of the
doctrines of state and society for which Western thought is indebted to de Tocqueville.

Bryce's criticism may perhaps be apt, that de Tocqueville's
investigation of American conditions was undertaken with too
slight a previous knowledge of English social institutions; for
these, indeed, often account for the origin of the former. I am not
able to enter into a controversy on this point with so eminent an
authority on English-American constitutional theory. I am, however, inclined to believe that the whole tenor of *Democracy in
America,* proceeding as it does from an analysis of new-English
basic principles, is a refutation of Bryce's criticism. However that
may be, de Tocqueville would certainly be obliged to concede to
the English critic that at the present day, and even in 1901 when
James Bryce published the revised edition of his study of de
Tocqueville, he underestimated the power of the Union government, and that the American president is certainly (*vide* this
present year 1939) no "comparatively weak official" (James
Bryce, op. cit., p. 399). On the other hand there is today a decided improvement upon the maladministration and corruption
in municipal affairs which obtained in 1901, and with which facts
Bryce was then able legitimately to counter de Tocqueville's
theories. Furthermore, there are today no grounds for the sweeping assertion made by Bryce in 1901 that political parties in the
United States have more importance than legislative and executive bodies. For some decades a new permanent officialdom has
been in process of development which does not resign in a body
whenever a new president is elected.

It is true that further complications arise from the very fact of
the appearance of this new American professional officialdom.

Should the president attempt a "radical" policy affecting the framework of the United States constitution, these officials can adopt, with an eye to his successor, filibustering tactics, more or less apparent, and can thus wreck the president's policy. Finally, when the president comes to consider his re-election, which conventionally cannot occur more than twice,[2a] he is more dependent on party politics than is desirable for his political executive functions. For the president of the United States is not only head of the state, but at the same time head of the government, and, last but not least, responsible leader of his party, with which a second party is contending for power.

These are problems which de Tocqueville could not foresee in 1835, and we think it unjust to measure *Democracy in America* by the yardstick of knowledge not available till the present day. Since de Tocqueville wrote his book, America has long been entirely colonized, a capitalistic structure has spanned its length and breadth, and the number of its inhabitants has increased tenfold.

The abiding importance of de Tocqueville's book in face of these major transformations is due to one determining cause, namely, that its main accent does not lie on generalizations drawn from any one particular historical situation, de Tocqueville's whole concern having been the presentation of the structural features of a democratic order of society. His purpose was to gain comprehension of the institutions and philosophy of a democratic society, of which American appeared to him to be the example *par excellence*. This designation of America is still valid up to the present time, since the basic elements of democracy have by no means disappeared, but have become welded into the traditions of American life.

Protestants who would not bow to papal supremacy as well as democratic republicans laid the foundations of America on free land whose soil is rich in treasure. Their experience and puritanical industry have made possible the creation of institutions which bear indeed the impress of their home lands, but are free from the age-old European blood-feuds and unburdened by its traditional privileges. Chiefly important was the absence of an *aristocracy* in the new American society. De Tocqueville was constrained to describe a nation forged from such elements as "by far the most successful and durable form of democratic government that has yet appeared in the world" (Bryce, op. cit., p. 425).

In a letter which is so important that it must be quoted at length, de Tocqueville defined the "political aim" of his work for his friend Eugène Stoffels as follows: "I have sought to show what a democratic people is in our days, and by this delineation, executed with vigorous accuracy, my design has been to produce a twofold effect on my contemporaries. To those who make to themselves an ideal democracy, a brilliant vision which they think it easy to realize, I undertake to show that they have arrayed their future in false colours; that the democratic government they advocate, if it be of real advantage to those who can support it, has not the lofty features they ascribe to it; and, moreover, that this government can only be maintained on certain conditions of intelligence, private morality, and religious faith, which we do not possess; and that its political results are not to be obtained without labour.

"To those for whom the word 'democracy' is synonymous with disturbance, anarchy, spoliation, and murder, I have attempted to show that the government of democracy may be reconciled with respect for property, with deference for rights, with safety to freedom, with reverence to religion; that, if democratic government is less favourable than another to some of the finer parts of human nature, it has also great and noble elements; and that perhaps, after all, it is the will of God to shed a lesser grade of happiness on the totality of mankind (*de répandre un bonheur médiocre sur la totalité des hommes*), not to combine a greater share of it on a smaller number, or to raise the few to the verge of perfection. I have undertaken to demonstrate to them that, whatever their opinion on this point may be, it is too late to deliberate, that society is advancing and dragging them along with itself towards equality of conditions; that the sole remaining alternative lies between evils henceforth inevitable; that the question is not whether aristocracy or democracy can be maintained, but whether we are to live under a democratic society, devoid indeed of poetry and greatness, but at least orderly and moral, or under a democratic society, lawless and depraved, abandoned to the frenzy of revolution, or subjected to a yoke heavier than any of those which have crushed mankind since the fall of the Roman Empire. I have sought to calm the ardour of the former class of persons, and, without discouragement, to point out the only path before them. I have sought to allay the terrors of the latter, and to bend their minds to the idea of an inevitable future, so that with less impetuosity on the one hand, and less resistance on the other, the world may advance more peaceably to the necessary fulfilment of its destiny. This is the fundamental idea of the book; an idea which connects all its other ideas in a single web. There are, however, as yet very few persons who understand the book. Many people of opposite opinions are pleased with it, not because they understand me, but because they find in my book, considered on one side only, certain arguments favourable to their own passion of the moment. But I have confidence in the future, and hope the day will come when everybody will see clearly what a few only perceive at present. . . ."[3]

It is apparent from this passage that de Tocqueville was not in the least dazzled by the material success of his book. To the satisfaction of the Conservatives he had warned the Liberals against exaggerated enthusiasm for the democratic state, and, in the other direction, to the great contentment of the Liberals, he had pointed out to the Conservatives the providential legitimacy of the democratic social order. De Tocqueville had subscribed to no party. He stood above parties, a Liberal of a new kind, a Conservative who perceived with glowing clarity the appropriate order of society in the modern Western world.

The prodigious success which had attended the work on America has already been noted. It was underlined in 1836 by an award of eight thousand francs from the Académie Française. De Tocqueville could well use this sum, for he had often been troubled by the financial worries which almost invariably attend the creation of a great intellectual work amid the leveling-down effect of modern mass society. "You know what are my theories on this point" (money worries), he writes to Count Gobineau (author of *The Inequality of Human Races,* a book de Tocqueville much disliked). "There is in our day only one kind of strength which is lasting, it is that proceeding from character. Only in one way can one be certain of preserving one's character intact, and that is by never feeling the need of money. *Ergo,* my conclusion is that if one cannot augment one's income one must learn to limit one's expenses."[4] De Tocqueville was no modern tuft-hunter, nor could he be deceived by the numerical superiority in editions achieved by his book over those of contemporary authors. Two years later he was nominated member of the Académie des Sciences Morales et Politiques, and in 1841 he joined the ranks of the forty "Immortals" of the Académie Française.

In the meantime the last volume of *Democracy in America* had appeared. De Tocqueville had worked at this final volume of his great book for five years; he published it in 1840. A comparison of this volume with the first two shows its undoubted superiority; the line of thought is more concise and more profound, the style more mature and polished; his range of view had become more universal. It cannot, however, be said that the book shared the enthusiastic reception of the first two volumes. It was, according to Gustave de Beaumont, not less purchased but less read. This is easily explained, for subject and method were too novel. Indeed, before de Tocqueville, who would have undertaken to show, in addition to its influence on political affairs, the interconnection of the democratic order of society with the intellectual, emotional, and moral substance of a nation? Machiavelli, Bodin, Rousseau, and Montesquieu undoubtedly initiated such an enterprise, but none of these four great modern predecessors of de Tocqueville had at his disposal so extensive and sure a knowledge of that "logic of the heart" (*ordre du cœur*) whose precepts had been rediscovered by the acute mind of Pascal, and by the deeply religious feeling of the Jansenists. Only Aristotle's *Politics,* based as it was securely on the inherent political sense of the Greek, was able to harmonize the moral forces of mankind with the nature of political institutions. None of the newer political philosophers equaled de Tocqueville in his appreciation of the idea of the totality of political man in the Greek sense, enriched now by the dawning modern mass state. A possible exception is Thomas Hobbes, whose naturalistic-mechanistic psychology, however, obscured for him phenomena which de Tocqueville found brilliantly portrayed in such great French moralists as La Rochefoucauld, La Bruyère, Vauvenargues, and, above all, in Pascal.

Analysis is only profitable when things have first been seen and experienced in their living totality. Herein lay the unique greatness of Pascal, whom de Tocqueville followed in applying to the political existence of man Pascal's own method of viewing moral phenomena in connection with their appropriate categories.

De Tocqueville, however, was not only without true predecessors; he was without true successors. The method and substance of the third volume of *Democracy in America* is today still conpletely unknown, although John Stuart Mill has described the book, with profound truth, in his notice of the complete work, as "the first philosophical book ever written on Democracy as it manifests itself in modern society; a book, the essential doctrines of which it is not likely that any future speculations will subvert, to whatever degree they may modify them; while its spirit, and the general mode in which it treats its subject, constitute the beginning of a new era in the scientific study of politics."[5] The validity of Mill's judgment remains unimpaired to the present day.

Of the last volume of *Democracy in America* we touch here only upon the fourth part, for it contains the synthesis and quintessence of de Tocqueville's work.

Democratic revolution is the hallmark of the age. The future, according to de Tocqueville's prediction, made at the end of the fourth decade of the nineteenth century, belongs to equality. In former centuries certain rights were granted to cities, to families, and to individuals, but in the great modern mass societies, brought into being by increasing industrialization, all citizens will face one another as *equals*. These men of the new age hold simple and general ideas; like their philosophy, their religion, their intelligence, and their government—the supreme authority of their state—must be simple and undivided. They regard uniformity in law as the hallmark of good government. The individual becomes lost in the mass and fixes his eyes solely on the mighty and all-embracing vision of the people as a whole.

Filled with pride and self-reliance among his equals, man will at first imagine that independence to be freedom. Because all men are visibly becoming equal, this very feeling of freedom may impel modern mankind to political anarchy, although, more probably, it will lead to servitude with the rise of some leader who will ruthlessly make himself master of these competing equalities. To the equal citizen the power of the state seems to be the one and only support of his own individual weakness. It is in these conditions that de Tocqueville perceives the most formidable danger to democratic communities, and it may be asserted without fear of exaggeration that it is on this especial aspect that de Tocqueville concentrates his political doctrine.

On the other hand (as de Tocqueville maintains) the power of the state favors the equality of citizens because this secures and extends its dominion. "I am of opinion," he writes, "that in the democratic ages which are opening upon us, individual independence and local liberties will ever be the product of artificial contrivance; that centralization will be the natural form of government."[6] This thesis may easily be proved from history. The English Puritans who emigrated in the seventeenth century to found a democratic commonwealth on the shores of the New World carried with them the liberties to which they were accustomed. They had learned to take a part in public affairs in their mother country, they took for granted independent administration of justice, their religious beliefs, and their ideas about liberty of speech and of the press. They defended these free institutions against the encroachments of the state. The example of Napoleon I, on the other hand, shows that he was forced, after destroying the nobility and the upper middle classes, to center in his own hands all the administrative functions of the state. In this case, in contrast to the example of America, the guarantees of individual freedom were annihilated. De Tocqueville brilliantly formulates the basic orders of American, English, and French social life in the following words: "The lot of the Americans is singular; they have derived from the aristocracy of England the notion of private rights and the taste for local freedom: and they have been able to retain both the one and the other because they have had no aristocracy to combat."[7]

The tendency to the centralization of government is irresistible. It is common to all the political communities of Europe. The privileges of the nobility, the liberties of cities, and the powers of provincial bodies are either destroyed or on the verge of destruction. Uniformity prevails in the modern world. De Tocqueville sees that even religions, both Protestant and Catholic, are in danger from the new powers of the state. States often make the clergy their servants, "and by this alliance with religion they reach the inner depths of the soul of man."[8] In the last volume of his work de Tocqueville shows that the threatening "new despotism" (Lord Hewart) of bureaucracy has by no means escaped his attention. In a note (pp. 499 *et seq.*) he writes as follows: "In proportion as the duties of the central power are augmented, the number of public officials (*fonctionnaires*) by whom that power is represented must increase also. They form a nation within each nation; and as they share the stability of the Government, they more and more fill up the place of an aristocracy."

This, however, is by no means a complete picture of the new Leviathan as prophetically envisaged by deTocqueville. With the increasing centralization of the power of the state it becomes also more inquisitorial and more detailed (*plus inquisitive et plus détaillée*): "It everywhere interferes in private concerns more than it did; it regulates more undertakings, and undertakings of a lesser kind; and it gains a firmer footing every day, about, above, and around all private persons, to assist, to advise, and to coerce them."[9] The economic activity of the modern state is also on the increase, the government becoming not only the country's chief industrialist, but tending to invade the domain of many private industrial enterprises, and to bring them forcibly under its control.

It is manifestly a very peculiar dialectic which is moving modern society. De Tocqueville defines its laws as follows: "As long as the democratic revolution was glowing with heat the men who were bent upon the destruction of old aristocratic powers hostile to that revolution displayed a strong spirit of independence; but as the victory of the principle of equality became more complete, they gradually surrendered themselves to the propensities natural to that condition of equality, and they strengthend and centralized their governments. *They had sought to be free in order to make themselves equal; but in proportion as equality was more established by the aid of freedom, freedom itself was thereby rendered more difficult of attainment.*"[10] (The italics are ours.)

I believe that de Tocqueville has revealed the very structure of the modern mass society in this dialectical exposition. It might certainly be said that he has merely condensed into an abstract formula the historical dynamics of the French Revolution. Undoubtedly he regarded the French Revolution as the classical example of this historical process. He traced the stages of this process in the period of development from July 14, 1789, to the Caesarism of Napoleon I. As we have seen, however, he by no means regarded the French Revolution of 1789–1815 as finally concluded then, but only as the first unitary stage of a revolutionary cycle destined to repeat itself with growing intensity in accordance with the growing industrialization of the modern world.

Most earnestly and in varying terms de Tocqueville reiterates his conviction that the species of depotism by which democratic nations are menaced is a *new* phenomenon for which there is no historical analogy. "The thing itself is new; and since I cannot name it, I must attempt to define it."[11]

He envisages a multitude of men, all equal and alike, working in order to procure for themselves petty and paltry pleasures. The age of "facilities" which Goethe apprehensively prophesied has set in. Above the race of mankind rises a monstrous tutelary power which "provides for their security, foresees and supplies their necessities, facilitates their pleasures, directs their industry, regulates the descent of property, and subdivides their inheritance—what remains but to spare them all the care of thinking and all the trouble of living?"[12] Thus each nation is reduced to the condition of a flock of timid and industrious animals, of which the government is the shepherd. Aldous Huxley's *Brave New World* stands before us! Today, perhaps, de Tocqueville would call such a democracy a "prebliscitary dictatorship," and would recognize its living image in the Fascist states! The grandeur of his prophetic gift is impressed upon one by the fact that after the passage of a hundred years his words have proved an exact description of a present-day reality.

How can the modern mass society escape this new despotism? "All those of our contemporaries who would establish or secure the independence and the dignity of their fellow-men, must show themselves the friends of equality, and the only worthy means of showing themselves as such, *is to be so:* upon this depends the success of their holy enterprise."[13]

De Tocqueville once again underlines the essential institutional requirements offering a possible counterpoise to the threat of despotism—secondary administrative bodies (both municipal and provincial) with elected officials, independent courts of law, freedom of the press, and parliamentary inviolability. In reference to the freedom of the press de Tocqueville however, makes one reservation of particular significance for the present day and one which, I believe, there has been a tendency to overlook. "I think that men living in aristocracies may, strictly speaking, do without the liberty of the press: but such is not the case with those who live in democratic countries. To protect their personal independence I trust not to great political assemblies, to parliamentary privileges, or to the assertion of popular sovereignty. All these things may, to a certain extent, be reconciled with personal servitude—but that servitude cannot be complete if the press is free: the press is the chiefest democratic instrument of freedom."[14] De Tocqueville, in stating his belief that in the case of an aristocratic community the freedom of the press can be dispensed with, again betrays in no uncertain manner his instinctive bias in favor of the nobility. Indeed, he himself admits it as we have seen above, that for him the traditions of a natural elite are sufficient guarantee of a free order of society.

To lay down distinct and definite limits to the already widely extended power of the government is de Tocqueville's main concern, for only so can individual man in the modern mass society hope to maintain whatever private rights he still possesses. "I wish the rulers would try a little more to make great men; that they would set less value on the work, and more upon the workman; that they would never forget that a nation cannot long remain strong when every man belonging to it is individually weak, and that no form or combination or social policy has yet been devised to make an energetic people of a community of pusillanimous and enfeebled citizens."[15]

On this note of high exhortation we can conclude our brief survey of *Democracy in America*—a work[16] which secures for de Tocqueville for all time the rank of one of the greatest amongst the political thinkers of the West.

FIVE

Politics: Venture and Dilemma

An iron consistency ruled de Tocqueville's life. A thinker who, in his thirtieth year, was able to plot out the future social evolution of the nations of the West—an enterprise only possible through his truly profound analysis of American democracy—would not and could not confine himself to political theory alone, but was bound to test it in practice. He had proved himself as a teacher of political science—one of the greatest in the history of political philosophy—and now he had to try out his own doctrine. It was for this that de Tocqueville threw himself into the political activities of his day.

While he was still working upon the final volume of his book on America he put up as candidate for his native constituency, the *arrondissement* of Valognes (La Manche). Since his mother's death he had lived in the ancestral castle at Tocqueville, apportioned to him by agreement with his two elder brothers. In 1837 he made his first bid for election as deputy.

Count Molé, Louis Philippe's prime minister (and incidentally a relation of de Tocqueville's), was willing enough to smooth the already famous young political scientist's way into politics, but de Tocqueville firmly declined such assistance. He wanted to be elected without previous parliamentary commitments, feeling that the "independent position" he wished to occupy as a deputy was possible only if he owed his seat entirely to his own efforts. Naturally enough he failed at the polls, but his honest repudiation of government support procured him election two years later with an overwhelming majority. De Tocqueville remained deputy for the *arrondissement* of Valognes from 1839 to 1851. In the Chamber he "sided consistently with the constitutional opposition" (Gustave de Beaumont).

At the same time, that is from 1842 to 1848, de Tocqueville was a member of the Conseil Général de la Manche, on which he represented the cantons of Sainte-Mère-Église and Montebourg. Since in 1933 Édmond L'Hommedé did the service of publishing de Tocqueville's notes and speeches on this council we are in a position to get a clear view of his work upon it. Of special interest are the documents which throw light on his attitude to the problem of foundling children, his emphatic support of a direct railway line from Caen to Cherbourg, and a brilliant historic, economic, military, and political analysis of the importance of the harbor of Cherbourg. All these papers are distinguished by thorough grasp of detail, a complete mastery of the politically possible, and not least a rare sense of social and humanitarian responsibility.

It was not in vain that de Tocqueville taught the absolute necessity of autonomous local administration for the health of a democratic state. His own example shows how significant and fruitful was the political experience acquired within a smaller communal unit. De Tocqueville never lost touch with his native place in Normandy, and his villagers loved him as grateful children love a kind father.

It is no part of our purpose here to give a detailed account of de Tocqueville's parliamentary activities. This task must be left for some future research worker, and it is to be hoped it may be undertaken soon. His work as a politician concerns us here only in so far as it is linked with his political doctrines. De Tocqueville was undoubtedly a prominent parliamentary worker, but he was not an important political leader. He may not have foreseen this very clearly at the beginning of his political career, and perhaps he may have hoped to exercise a visible and decisive influence on the history of his country. But it is certain that he must soon have realized that great political leaders are made of other stuff. With a ruthless self-analysis, reminiscent again of Pascal, he perceived this: he was neither a persuasive speaker nor a brilliant debater. His parliamentary speeches, delivered after careful written preparation, are very well-thought-out expositions of certain political and administrative reforms which the constitutional opposition endeavored to force upon Guizot's cabinet during its period of office from 1840 until the February revolution. In 1839 de Tocqueville was appointed by a committee of which he was a member to report on their investigations of the treatment of slaves in the French colonies. In 1840 he became member of a commission on prison reform. In 1846 he had to deal with African colonial problems, for the study of which he had made two journeys to Algiers. On one of these journeys he fell dangerously ill. His most important speech was made on January 29, 1848, a month before the outbreak of the February revolution, when he vainly prophesied to the Chamber the coming upheaval. A few pivotal passages from this speech must be quoted here:

". . . A time is coming when the country will once again find itself divided into two great parties. The French Revolution, which abolished all privileges and destroyed all exclusive rights, has yet left one which subsists throughout the land—the right of property. But property-owners need cherish no illusions as to the strength of their position, nor need they fancy that the right of property is an unassailable bulwark because it has never yet been reached—for our times are unlike any others. As long as the right of property was the origin and groundwork of many other rights it was easily defended—or rather it was not attacked; it was then the citadel of society, while all the other rights were its outworks; it did not bear the brunt of attack and, indeed, there was no serious attempt to assail it. But to-day, when the right of property is regarded as the last undestroyed remnant of the aristocratic world, when it alone is left standing, the sole privilege in an equalized society . . . it is a very different matter. . . . Consider what is passing in the hearts of the working classes, although I admit they are quiet enough as yet. It is true that they are less inflamed than formerly by political passions, properly speaking;

but do you not see that their passions, from being *political* have become *social?* [our italics]. Do you not see that little by little, ideas and opinions are spreading amongst them which aim not merely at removing such and such laws, such a ministry or such a government, *but at breaking up the very foundations of society itself?* [our italics]. . . . Such, gentlemen, is my deepest conviction: I believe that at this very moment we are sleeping on a volcano—I am profoundly convinced of it. . . .

"When I come to seek in different ages, different epochs, different peoples, for the effective cause that has led to the ruin of their governing classes, I see, indeed, such and such a man, such and such an event, such and such an accidental or superficial cause, but, believe me, the true cause, the effective cause of men's loss of power, is that they become unworthy to wield it."[1]

Four weeks later the February revolution broke out in Paris and became the prelude to a European movement whose momentum, following laws proclaimed by de Tocqueville, has continued down to our own day. De Tocqueville did not, however, prophesy alone. In 1842 Lorenz von Stein foresaw social revolution in the very near future, while both Marx and Engels in the *Communist Manifesto* (whose composition preceded de Tocqueville's speech by only a few months) recognized in the social antagonism between bourgeoisie and proletariat the basic problem of the coming decades.

The charge has been brought against de Tocqueville that during his parliamentary career his political bearing showed little sign of that "new sort of liberalism" which we have endeavored to characterize above. This reproach is, in our opinion, scarcely justified. De Tocqueville began with too much knowledge of the workaday political machine to make any attempt to correct "the clumsy commonplaces which direct and rule the world" by unintelligibly delicate distinctions. His sole—and well-justified—claim, in a parliament rendered for the most part corrupt and therefore complaisant by the Guizot government, was to the good faith, the solid and statesmanlike insight, which distinguished him and his few friends even from the rest of the opposition led by Adolphe Thiers.

De Tocqueville was at heart unable to give his unreserved assent and support to the French liberalism of his day. In a remarkable letter of March 22, 1837, to his friend Henry Reeve, translator of his book on America, he describes his attitude to political party. "My critics insist upon making me out a partyman; but I am not that. Passions are attributed to me where I have only opinions; or rather I have but one opinion, an enthusiasm for liberty and for the dignity of the human race. I consider all forms of government merely as so many more or less perfect means of satisfying this holy and legitimate craving. People ascribe to me alternately aristocratic and democratic prejudices. If I had been born in another period, or in another country, I might have had either the one or the other. But my birth, as it happened, made it easy for me to guard against both. I came into the world at the end of a long revolution, which after destroying ancient institutions, created none that could last. When I entered life, aristocracy was dead and democracy was yet unborn. My instinct, therefore, could not lead me blindly either to the one or to the other. I lived in a country which for forty years had tried everything and settled nothing. I was on my guard, therefore, against political illusions. Belonging myself to the ancient aristocracy of my country, I had no natural hatred or jealousy of the aristocracy; nor could I have any natural affection for it, since that aristocracy had ceased to exist, and one can be strongly attached only to the living. I was near enough to know it thoroughly, and far enough to judge it dispassionately. I may say as much for the democratic element. It had done me, as an individual, neither good nor evil. I had no personal motive, apart from my public convictions, to love or to hate it. Balanced between the past and the future, with no natural instinctive attraction towards either, I could without an effort quietly contemplate each side of the question."[2] This passage might easily, though mistakenly, be regarded as contradicting the confession quoted just previously in which de Tocqueville describes himself as "an aristocrat by instinct." I hold, however, that there is no contradiction between the two passages, since what de Tocqueville disclaims in his letter to Reeve is only a *class* attachment to the aristocracy—a thing impossible to one who saw through the aristocratic ideology so completely. The aristocracy to which de Tocqueville adhered was that "nobility" illumined by Goethe's and Jacob Burckhardt's dread of the approaching mass age. Such an attitude in de Tocqueville was a matter of course—and constant. He gave it moving expression in a letter to a friend shortly before his death, in which he wrote: ". . . we belong to a moral and intellectual family which is disappearing."[3] De Tocqueville saw no escape from the leveling-down process inherent in his own period and in the future.

Although the letter to Henry Reeve is clearly intended as a critical refutation of misinterpretations of the book on America, it may be rightly regarded as having a bearing on de Tocqueville's attitude to the political parties of Louis Philippe's parliament. Political common sense prevented de Tocqueville from pressing his isolation to the limit. Parliamentary politics are impossible without a measure of compromise in principle, and the author of *Democracy in America* could have no doubts on the point, but in all the political engagements which he was forced to enter into he never surrendered absolutely his individual right of judgment. Writing to his wife in 1842, just after entering the new Chamber, he says: "The Chamber, as I told you, is very like its predecessor. There are two large, equal parties; between them there is a handful of trimmers, who accord the victory alternately to one side or to the other. My own attitude is almost the same. I have done nothing considerable. Several of the new deputies, persons of merit, seem to want to stand in with us. I have no faith in the future of these associations, but they work easily enough with new, as yet unclassed men. I lend myself to this without expecting much from it. The main point is, what proofs I can give of my capacity and my character. Have I either one or the other to an eminent degree? I am far from having proved this to myself. . . ."[4] We owe much to Antoine Redier for giving us this hitherto unpublished letter, for it plainly shows us de Tocqueville's very self—revealed without reserve to the wife he loved. An ardent political ambition—one might call it an objective ambition—filled the young politician, yet that very same year he came near to answering his own question in the negative. In a letter of November 22, 1842, to Gustave de Beaumont, he writes: "You drive me to despair when you speak of a great part for me. I know better than any one what I lack for a part of that kind—self-confidence, to begin with. Moreover, what good can you expect on this Dead Sea of politics? The great parts in politics need great passions to fill them. No man can battle with *éclat* against apathy, indifference, and an entire nation's discouragement. In vain I pile up a great fire in my imagination; I feel all about me a chill that penetrates every part of me; do what I will it extinguishes the word in me."[5] Three years of parliamentary experience had left de Tocqueville the victim of a profound melancholy, a comfortless sense of hollowness, even in the midst of practical activity. In 1839 Lamartine, speaking of the changing cabinets of the Citizen King, declared that "France is a *bored* nation," and it was not otherwise under Guizot's regime when de Tocqueville remarked: "How can the country be prevented from falling little by little into profound apathy?"[6]

Thiers, leader of the liberal opposition in the Chamber, appeared to him the very protoype of dishonesty and intrigue in politics. It was torment to him to have to try to come to a mutual understanding with this man, his contrast in all respects, and confidential letters to his friends Beaumont and Kergorlay show this. "I lack the qualities," writes de Tocqueville in 1842, "to play a leading part in the Chamber at the present time; and I cannot see one man whom I esteem enough to follow. This would seem to condemn me to a fruitless isolation which makes me despair. I need a further apprenticeship, but how and under whom? . . ."[7]

Ultimately his only teachers were the passing years and his own inner nature. In his *Souvenirs* he gives a vivid picture of parliamentarianism under the Citizen King. "What was principally lacking in a political world thus composed and ordered, especially towards its close, was political life itself. This could scarcely be either born or nourished within the legal circle marked out by the constitution; the ancient nobility was vanquished, the people was excluded. As all business was transacted between the members of a single class, in its interests and in its spirit, it was not possible to find a battleground where great parties could strive with each other. The singular homogeneity of position, interests, and consequently of views, which prevailed in what M. Guizot called the *pays légal* [legal land] deprived parliamentary debates of all originality, all reality, all genuine passion. I have spent ten years of my life in the company of men of very high intelligence who constantly exerted themselves without ever growing warm, and who employed all their perspicacity to discover subjects of controversy without ever finding them.

"Furthermore, the preponderance which King Louis Philippe had acquired in the business of government meant that no one could diverge far from that prince's ideas without loss of power, and this reduced the party colours to mere *nuances,* and the party struggle to quarrels over words. I doubt if any parliament . . . has ever comprised more varied and brilliant talents than did ours during the last years of the July Monarchy. Yet I can affirm that great orators grew bored of listening to one another there, and, worse still, the entire nation grew bored of listening to them. Insensibly the country accustomed itself to regard the struggles in the Chambers rather as intellectual exercises than as serious discussions, and the party divisions—majority, left centre, or legitimist opposition—as childish family squabbles. A few startling instances of corruption, accidentally brought to light, created the impression that more were hidden, that the whole governing class was corrupt, and resulted in a cool public contempt which was mistaken for confident submission and satisfaction.

"The country was at that time divided into . . . two equal zones: in the higher, which alone ought to contain the whole political life of the nation, there was nothing but langour, weakness, inertia, boredom: in the lower, on the contrary, the beginnings of a political life were manifest in feverish symptoms and irregularities plain to any attentive observer."[8] Not Marx himself, who in his *Eighteenth Brumaire of Louis Bonaparte* has given us a brilliant picture of the social causes which led to the French revolution of 1848, would have had anything to object to this description of de Tocqueville's.

Under the census government of Guizot no more than two hundred thousand persons were enfranchised out of a total population approaching thirty-five million. These figures prove that de Tocqueville's picture of parliamentarianism at the time of the July monarchy is in no way exaggerated: such was "the legal land" of Guizot's creation. When pressed to create a juster franchise Guizot said, significantly: "Work and grow rich and you will become voters."[9] Guizot, more of a retrospective historian than a politician, thought universal franchise an absurd system; to concede the exercise of political rights to every living person was an idea quite unacceptable to him.

It was inevitable that de Tocqueville should feel a stranger in such a world as this, and the February revolution of 1848 must have meant for him relief from a monstrous burden. He foresaw it more clearly than any of his contemporaries. Within twenty-four hours the bourgeois monarchy of the *Enrichissez-vous* crumbled to pieces. Louis Philippe managed to escape to England. In Paris a provisional government was formed in which for the first time socialist leaders took a part.

We need not enter here into the details of the course of the '48 in France.[10] On February 24 the workers of Paris boasted of having dismissed the king and his hated government, but they were enabled to win this "victory" only through the supineness of the petty-bourgeois National Guards: even the army was scarcely touched by the change. The general staff and the officers appeared to recognize the newly formed democratic republic, but their true attitude was revealed only with the rise to power of Louis Napoleon.

The elections for the National Assembly, which took place on April 23, and which again returned de Tocqueville to parliament, plainly showed in what way the forces of class had ranged themselves in the interval. The provisional government had, indeed, extended the franchise to almost nine and a half millions, but, on the other hand, by setting up the so-called National Workshops of Paris at the instigation of Louis Blanc for dealing with unemployment, they had shown too "red" a tendency. Added to this there was a foolish decree which raised the Land Tax by 45 per cent and made the peasant small-holders and bourgeois landowners bear the burden of the insolvency of the Parisian government. The result of the polls showed a bourgeois-republican majority of five hundred members as against a strong monarchist opposition of three hundred; the socialists' party held only a hundred seats out of the total of nine hundred in all.

It was plain that the young French socialist party had met defeat at the polls. On June 23, 1848, there was a further uprising of the Parisian proletariat, but it was a hopeless effort from the start, and was crushed by General Cavaignac, who appeared as the "savior" of society and private property, after three days of bloody conflict.

In these first days of revolution de Tocqueville was naturally not to be found on the side of the workers' class. His penetrating and independent mind had indeed foretold the approaching *social* changes in France's political revolution. In a masterly passage of the *Souvenirs* he analyzes the socialistic tendencies of the February revolution as follows: "Although the working classes often played the principal part in the events of the first Revolution, they have never been the leaders and sole masters of the State, either *de facto* or *de jure;* probably not a single man of the people sat in the Convention, which was filled with the bourgeoisie and with literary men. The war between the Montagnards and the Girondists was fought on both sides by members of the bourgeoisie, and the victory of the former did not permit power to fall into the hands of the people alone. The July revolution was made by the people, but the middle class instigated and directed it, and reaped its chief fruits. The February revolution, on the contrary, appeared to be made entirely apart from and against the bourgeoisie.

"In the great shock of conflict the two parties which principally composed the social body of France became in some sort detached, and the people alone were left in possession of power. This was a thing utterly new in our annals; analogous revolutions have occurred it is true, in other countries and other ages, for the history of our own times, however new and unforeseen it may appear, is but a part of human history as it has existed from the beginning, and what we call new facts are most often only old facts forgotten."[11] This passage affords insight into de Tocqueville's characteristic habit of thought. He sees the February revolution as a phase of French social history (indeed, of Western social development in general), and he formulates, as it were in passing, one of the basic principles of his historical philosophy which we shall have occasion to examine later in this book. In the *Souvenirs* he continues as follows: "Notably Florence, towards the close of the Middle Ages, presented in little a spectacle similar to our own; the nobles were at first succeeded by the bourgeois class, which in its turn was displaced from governmental power, and a bare-foot *gonfalonnier* marched at the head of the people and ruled the republic. But in Florence this revolution of the populace was the product of special and transitory causes, while here it was brought about by causes so lasting and so general that, after agitating France, it might well be believed they would stir up the whole of Europe. This time it was no question of the triumph of a party: men aspired to found a social science, a philosophy, I might almost say a religion, to be learned and followed by all mankind. Here something really new was added to the ancient picture."[12] The socialist leaders (as de Tocqueville makes clear in the *Souvenirs*) had undoubtedly shown themselves incapable of carrying through this new social revolution: "They did not understand either how to use, or how to do without, universal suffrage. If they had held the elections directly after 24th February while the upper classes were still stunned by the blow they had received, they might have got a parliament after their own hearts; if they had boldly seized the dictatorship they might have held it in their hands for some time. But they put themselves into the nation's hands, and at the same time did everything most calculated to estrange it; they menaced it at the same time that they surrendered to it; they frightened it by the boldness of their projects and the violence of their language while inviting resistance by the weakness of their acts; they gave themselves the airs of preceptors and at the same time made themselves dependents."[13] When seventy years later German Social Democracy was faced with a similar historic task its leaders showed that they had learned little from the experiences of the French February revolution. Actually, new events are always in essence merely a part of the same old human history, and what we call new events are all too often only forgotten events. The German Social-Democratic leaders in 1918 and later were, indeed, masters of forgetfulness.

De Tocqueville would certainly have given his political support to French socialism if he had believed that the socialistic movement of his day was in accord with the ideas, morals, and passions of the age. He never lacked courage, but he saw the socialist movement as a mere tendency which in the distant future of Western history might show itself stronger than in those spring days of 1848.

His decision was soon made. He would not stand for this government or for that but for the laws which constituted French society as such. His possessions, his peace, and his person weighed light with him while, as he believed, the very existence of the French state was at stake, and human dignity was in danger. Once again the *Souvenirs* give classic expression to what de Tocqueville conceived as his duty at the time. "To protect the ancient laws of society against innovators with the help of the new power with which the republican principle endows a government; to make the evident will of the French people triumph over the passions and desires of the workers of Paris; by so doing to conquer demagogy by democracy—such was my sole object. I have never had an aim at once so exalted and so plain to view."[14]

Democracy versus Demagogy—this was the banner under which de Tocqueville sought to serve. Shortly before the June rising he was voted on to the constitutional commission of the National Assembly. The great analyst of the American constitution thus obtained effective influence in the reformation of the French constitution.

The commission began its work with a discussion of communal decentralization, which de Tocqueville, as we have already seen, held to be one of the essentials of a democratic state. The discussion, however, brought out irreconcilable differences of opinion among the commissioners, so that the point was forthwith abandoned and the administrative centralization traditional in France remained untouched. There was more prolonged debate on the question of a one-chamber or a two-chamber system. De Tocqueville supported the setting-up of a two-chamber system, and Barrot backed him, but still he remained hopelessly outnumbered. It was accepted by the commission as axiomatic that the executive should be responsible to one chamber only. The question now arose as to how the supreme head of the republican state was to be chosen, and as to what constitutional limitations should be imposed on the president. Here, again, the commission worked too hastily without taking stock of all the possible consequences of this weighty problem. De Tocqueville had grave doubts about direct popular election of the president. Might not a president, elected by the people under the French system of centralization, which the revolution had not dared to touch, easily become a pretender to the throne? Louis Napoleon had recently been elected by Paris and three *départements* into the National Assembly. De Tocqueville's anxiety was but too well justified. "I remember," he says in the *Souvenirs,* "that all the time the commission was occupied with this business my mind was at work to discover on which side the balance of power ought habitually to lie in such a republic as I saw in the making; sometimes I thought it should lie with a single Assembly, sometimes with an elected president. This uncertainty troubled me greatly. Actually it was not possible to foresee how it would be; the victory of one or other of the two great rivals must depend on the circumstances and dispositions of the moment. *The only thing certain was that there would be war between them to the ruin of the republic"* [the italics are ours].[15] De Tocqueville wrote this account, after the event, at Sorrento in

March 1851 to clear his own mind and to leave a valuable lesson for posterity. Rather more than six months later Louis Napoleon's *coup d'état* put an end to the Second French Republic, even as de Tocqueville had prophesied. Of the remaining work of the commission perhaps only its rescue of the principle that judges should not be subject to dismissal deserves mention. Later, de Tocqueville regarded this as the one achievement of the 1848 commission which was certain to endure.

The commission's task was rushed through in less than a month and it gave de Tocqueville no satisfaction. The times were too unsettled, the necessities of the day too urgent, to give scope for thorough work. "One and all," writes de Tocqueville (in the *Souvenirs*) of these constitution-builders of the Second Republic, "they were very unlike those men, so sure of their aim, so much in command of the methods to be used to attain it, who, under Washington's presidency, drew up the American constitution sixty years ago."[16] Yet for a man like de Tocqueville, who had a vision of the totality of the political sphere, these weeks must have afforded valuable study, not least in ripening his ideas on the relationship between political theory and political practice.

On December 10, 1848, Louis Napoleon was elected president of the Republic by an overwhelming majority. De Tocqueville had supported Cavaignac. On May 13, 1849, a new national legislative assembly was elected. De Tocqueville was returned again, although many of his friends failed to retain their seats. The socialists were stronger in the new parliament, holding a hundred and fifty seats. The conflicts of the previous June had found an echo in the country at large.

The cabinet was reconstructed, and on June 2 de Tocqueville was appointed foreign minister to the French Republic. "We wanted," we read in the *Souvenirs*, "to call the republic to life: he (the president) wanted to bury it. We were only his ministers, and he wanted accomplices."[17] This sentence completely sums up the situation, even though written in retrospect. The new minister took up his task with a sure hand. "I felt perplexed, worried, discouraged, agitated, in face of small responsibilities. I experienced mental tranquillity, a strange calm, when in the presence of very great ones. The sense of the importance of the things I was then doing lifted me at once to their level, and kept me there. Hitherto the thought of defeat had been insupportable to me, yet the vision of resounding disaster in the role I had now undertaken on one of the greatest of the world's stages troubled me not at all—proving to myself that my weakness was not that of timidity, but that of pride. . . ."[18] He appointed trusted friends to the embassies—Lamorcière to St. Petersburg, Corcelle to Rome, Beaumont to Vienna. On these men he could build securely.

His task was lightened by his unerring judgment of human beings. "My secret, if it must be told, consisted in flattering their *amour-propre* while I ignored their opinions."[19] He handled even de Broglie, Molé, and Thiers by this method, which he certainly had not needed to learn from Machiavelli. His ten years in the French parliament had not been in vain. Of the "great matters" with which his new office confronted him it is sufficient to mention the Piedmontese incident, the Turkish question, the Roman question, and the problem of the Swiss rights of asylum.

Nothing conclusive can be said about de Tocqueville's handling of the Roman question until his correspondence with Corcelle has been made accessible to the public, but the other issues give convincing proof of his statesmanlike action. Some ten thousand revolutionary fugitives from Germany, Austria, and Russia had found a temporary refuge in Switzerland: Friedrich Engels, among others, had fled there from Baden. These three states now threatened to exercise police rights in Switzerland unless she expelled these turbulent "red" elements. De Tocqueville supported France's menaced neighbor and ally by declaring that France would go to war before she would allow Switzerland to be bullied or humiliated by other powers. At the same time he had the French-Swiss frontier closed, so that France's democratic ally was obliged to expel revolutionaries regarded by France also as dangerous. De Tocqueville did not find it hard to combine national honor with political ends. In his account in the *Souvenirs* of the

Swiss dispute he comments significantly on the relation between foreign and home politics in a democratic state: "Never has it been clearer that it is the nature of democracies to have, for the most part, most confused or erroneous ideas on external affairs, and to decide questions of foreign policy on purely domestic considerations."[20] This sentence shows how deeply he had pondered the principles of his new office.

He acted similarly in the Austrian-Piedmontese conflict. Austria had defeated Piedmont at Novara and peace was practically concluded, but for a quite small financial indemnity due from Piedmont. Suddenly Austria raised her demands. Once more the French foreign minister made an immediate threat of armed force. He stationed the Lyons army corps at the foot of the Alps, and thus secured the withdrawal of the Austrian demands, in his opinion unjust.

The Turkish question was more complex and far-reaching, threatening to attain European dimensions. Here again an emigrant question was the original cause of trouble. Hungarian revolutionaries, Kossuth among them, and Polish officers had found refuge in Turkey. Kossuth and Denbinski had furthermore put themselves expressly under the protection of the French embassy. Austria and Russia now demanded that Turkey should hand over the revolutionary leaders, and this Turkey refused to do. Even in those days there were lands more Christian than the seemingly Christian states of Europe. Turkey refused to give up the refugees; Austria and Russia thereupon broke off diplomatic relations with Constantinople, and war was imminent. England stood on the side of Turkey. De Tocqueville sent his ambassador definite orders, yet with instructions to use caution. Finally the tsar gave way. De Tocqueville had proved completely that he was fit to play in the European concert of powers.

Numerous documents show that he envisaged a close alliance with England as the basis of French foreign policy. He regarded England as a great example of political wisdom and political moderation: the spirit of British policy had been evolved through centuries of cool, unsentimental statesmanship. "I need not tell you," writes de Tocqueville to his English friend, Greg, on April 16, 1854, "how happy I am about this alliance [between England and France]; I have always thought it the most desirable event that could happen. This alliance alone can safeguard not only the common freedoms of Europe, as you say, but also the future liberties of each European nation."[21] Since then this maxim of French foreign policy has been hardened on the battlefields of the last world war, and in the year 1939 it certainly needs no further commentary.

De Tocqueville adopted the traditional French political attitude toward Germany. In a conversation with Senior he remarked that it was not in France's interest to see the growth of a great military power on her very frontier. He therefore thought Palmerston's foreign policy too Prussophile. In the *Souvenirs*, however, in contradiction to this attitude, we find the thesis that "the union of all the Germanic races is desirable" as an effective counterpoise to the tsarist tyranny. When de Tocqueville wrote this, however, his term of office as foreign minister was already ended. It seems that from 1835 on de Tocqueville had a deep presentiment of the Russian danger. On the last pages of the *Democracy in America* we find a remarkable passage which shows how intimately de Tocqueville's political conceptions are based on his sociological insights. These often-quoted sentences are:

"There are at the present time two great nations in the world, which started from different points, but seem to tend towards the same end. I allude to the Russians and the Americans. Both of them have grown up unnoticed; and while the attention of mankind was directed elsewhere, they have suddenly placed themselves in the front rank among the nations, and the world learned of their existence and their greatness at almost the same time.

"All other nations seem to have nearly reached their natural limits, and they have only to maintain their power; but these are still in the act of growth. All the others have stopped, or continue to advance with extreme difficulty; these alone are proceeding with ease and celerity along a path to which no limit can be perceived. The American struggles against the obstacles that nature opposes to him; the adversaries of the Russian are men. The former combats the wilderness and savage life; the latter, civilization with all its arms. The conquests of the American are therefore gained by the plowshare; those of the Russian by the sword. The Anglo-American relies upon personal interest to accomplish his ends and gives free scope to the unguided strength and common sense of the people; the Russian centers all the authority of society in a single arm. The principal instrument of the former is freedom; of the latter, servitude. Their starting-point is different and their courses are not the same; yet each of them seems marked out by the will of Heaven to sway the destinies of half the globe."

These lines perhaps explain the contradiction in de Tocqueville's political thought as far as Germany is concerned. In addition, this contradiction also reveals an apprehension in his attitude toward Russia, an uncertainty which is today as disturbing as it was in 1850 when de Tocqueville wrote his *Recollections*.

On October 31, 1849, Louis Napoleon dismissed the Odilon-Barrot Government. "Our fall was due neither to public opinion nor to a parliamentary campaign," writes de Tocqueville; "the President was determined to rule alone and to regard his ministers as mere agents and creatures. He may be right in wishing this. I will not go into the question: but we could not serve him under such conditions."[22] Later Louis Napoleon made frequent vain attempts to secure de Tocqueville's statesmanlike services again, but a politician for whom human dignity and human freedom were axiomatic political conceptions could come to no pact with that ruler.

De Tocqueville had no illusions about the character of the president, and I cannot resist quoting the pen picture of his lord and master which the ex-minister drew in his *Souvenirs*. It is one of the finest from de Tocqueville's masterly hand, and not even Plutarch modeled his heroes more convincingly.

"He was very superior to what his earlier life and his rash enterprises might justly lead one to expect him to be. This was my first impression in intercourse with him. In this respect he disappointed his enemies, and perhaps even more his friends, if such a title may be given to the politicians who supported his candidature. The greater number of the latter chose him actually not for his good qualities but for his presumed mediocrity. They thought they would find him a tool which they could use at discretion and, when occasion arose, break at will. In this they were greatly mistaken.

"As a private person Louis Napoleon had certain attractive qualities; an amiable and easy disposition, a humane character, a gentle and even tender spirit, though one lacking in delicacy, great assurance in social intercourse, perfect simplicity, and a certain personal modesty co-existing with immense pride of descent. He was capable of feeling affection and of inspiring it in those about him. He had little conversation, and was a dull talker when he did speak. He had not the art of making others talk or of getting intimately *en rapport* with them. He lacked facility in self-expression, but he had literary habits and a certain vanity of authorship. His capacity for dissimulation, which was great as befitted a man who had passed his life in conspiracy, received singular reinforcement from the immobility of his features and the insignificance of his glance—for his eyes were spiritless and opaque, like those thick panes of glass in the windows of ships' cabins which let in the light, but through which one cannot see. Utterly careless of danger, he had a fine cold courage in days of crisis, and at the same time, as is common enough, he was very vacillating in his plans. One often saw him change his direction, advance, hesitate, draw back—to his own great disadvantage, for the nation had chosen him to dare all, and what it expected of him was boldness, not prudence. It is said that he was always much addicted to pleasures, of which he was not delicate in the choice. This passion for vulgar satisfactions, this liking for comforts, grew with the opportunities afforded by power. He squandered his energies daily on these things and even clipped and curtailed his ambition for their sake. He had an incoherent and confused mentality filled with grandiose, ill-ordered ideas, borrowed sometimes from the example of Napoleon, sometimes from

the theories of socialism, sometimes from memories of England
(where he had lived)—in fact from very various, and frequently
contradictory, sources. He had laboriously assembled these ideas
during solitary meditation, apart from contact with men and facts,
for he was by nature a day-dreamer and fantasist. But when he
was forced to leave these vague and vast regions and to apply his
mind within the limits of the particular occasion it was capable
of good judgment, sometimes of finesse and penetration, even indeed of a certain depth, but it was never sure, and it was always
ready to place some bizarre idea side by side with a true one.

"In general it was hardly possible to be with him long or intimately without discovering a little streak of madness running thus
through his common sense, and its appearance, constantly recall-
ing the escapades of his youth, served also to explain them.

"For the rest one may say that it was to his madness rather
than to his sense to which, thanks to circumstances, he owed his
success and his strength: for the world is a strange theatre. There
are times when the worst pieces are those which have the best
success. If Louis Napoleon had been a wise man, or a man of
genius, he would never have become president of the republic.

"He believed in his 'star'; believed himself the instrument of
fate, the man of destiny. I have always believed that he was really
convinced of his rights, and I doubt if Charles X was ever more
infatuated about his legitimacy than was Louis Napoleon about
his. The latter was as incapable as the former, moreover, of
rationalizing his faith, for while he had a kind of abstract adora-
tion for the people, he had little taste for liberty. His most characteristic and fundamental trait in matters political was his hate
and scorn for parliamentary assemblies. Constitutional monarchy
seemed to him a less tolerable form of government even than a
republic. The boundless pride he drew from his name was willing
to bow to the nation, but revolted at the idea of submission to the
influence of a Parliament.

"Before he came to power he had had time to reinforce the
natural inclination of mediocre princes for flunkeyism by the
habits of twenty years of conspiracy passed amidst low-class ad-

venturers, ruined and tarnished men, young debauchees—the only persons who during this period consented to serve him as boon-companions and accomplices. There showed even through his own good manners something that smacked of the adventurer and charlatan. He continued to take pleasure in such inferior company even when he was no longer compelled to seek it out. I believe that his difficulty in expressing his thoughts otherwise than in writing bound him to these people who had long been in touch with his ideas and familiar with his dreams, and that in general his inferiority in conversation made contact with men of intellect painful to him. He wanted above everything a devotion to his person and to his cause that seemed to owe its existence to that person and that cause—independent merit made him uneasy. He needed faithful believers in his star, vulgar worshippers of his fortunes.

"Such was the man whom the need of a leader and the power of a memory placed at the head of France."[23] Any attempt to build up a sociological typology of the political leader of this modern era of mass societies must certainly set out from the figure of Louis Napoleon. His victory illustrates for the first time in modern history the triumph of political ineptitude. As has been seen, the Second French Republic extended the franchise from two hundred thousand to more than nine million people, without the provision of any sort of political education for them. The new electorate, into whose hands the fate of the nation had been placed as it were overnight, were certainly incapable of following the fine distinctions of parliamentary deliberations. They did not even wish to do so, but willingly transferred their mandate to the bearer of a "great name"—or rather to the man who accorded with, and knew how to appeal to, their own mediocrity. Later the Chamber restricted the franchise again, but not to the *status quo* of the Guizot regime. Louis Napoleon, however, insisted on the reintroduction of that universal suffrage which had brought him into power. December 2, 1851, saw the end of the debate on this matter, as also on that of the re-electability of the president, a point of bitter conflict between the latter and the Chamber; the way for the empire now lay open.

In the subsequent history of France the lessons of the Napoleonic plebiscite were never forgotten. They not only brought de Tocqueville (as we shall see) to a clearer definition of his political views but also deeply influenced those of Proudhon and Georges Sorel. Outside France probably the only men to comprehend the terrible possibilities of the new "Napoleonic principle" were Walter Bagehot, Jacob Burckhardt, Bismarck, and Constantin Frantz. It was reserved for our own day to accord new honors to "plebiscitary democracy," when in Fascist Italy and National-Socialist Germany it came to be recognized as a useful instrument for the political integration of the masses.

Universal suffrage is a two-edged political institution. Only when it is limited and secured by other political institutions, such as those de Tocqueville has so forcibly described, can it function according to its original intention: unlimited by such means it swings over into tyranny. Aristotle uttered a profound truth when he wrote in his *Politics* that the horizon of human vision ought to decide the frontiers of the state. The problem with which the great modern mass state is confronted could not be stated more precisely.

We now come to the last chapter of Alexis de Tocqueville's active political career. After his dismissal from the post of foreign minister he felt exhausted, used up. Nevertheless, he undertook the important task of reporting on the findings of a commission set up by parliament to study the question of the re-eligibility of the president. His report is to be found in volume nine of the *Œuvres complètes*. He wanted the decision of the Second Republic on the question of presidential re-eligibility revised, although earlier he had expressly opposed re-eligibility. It is characteristic of his unusually honest political conscience that, writing in March 1851 at Sorrento, he should have recorded so frankly his share in a question so crucial in the history of the Second Republic. Giving an account of the above-mentioned committee of the National Assembly he writes: "Beaumont proposed that the president should not be re-eligible; I supported him keenly and the motion passed. Both of us made a great mistake on this occasion, and I believe *the consequences will be very grievous* [our italics—de Tocqueville wrote these words nine months before the *coup d'état*]. We have always been very much alive to the dangers threatening liberty and public morality from a re-eligible president, who would inevitably sooner or later employ in advance for his own re-election the immense possibilities of constraint or corruption which our laws and our customs put at the disposal of the chief of our executive. Our minds were not sufficiently quick and supple instantly to see that from the moment when it was decided that the citizens themselves should elect the president directly the evil was irreparable, and that to attempt to hinder the people in their choice was but to increase the evil. This vote and the great influence I had upon it is the most painful memory I have of that time."[24]

It is as well to know that even so great a master of political theory may make a mistake. The laws of the political world are more complex than the rules of mathematics. De Tocqueville could have learned nothing from Thomas Hobbes. When, however, nine months later, de Tocqueville advocated a revision of the constitution, his proposal did not receive the requisite majority; Louis Napoleon, assured of victory, dared the *coup d'état*.

At first the *coup d'état* of December 2, 1851, shocked all Europe. The legitimist governments of Russia, Austria, and Prussia saw in Louis Napoleon, in Bismarck's words, "an unauthorized adventurer," who had made himself master of France. The British foreign minister, Lord Palmerston, sent his ambassador too hasty instructions to recognize the *coup d'état*, whereat the prime minister, the crown, and the majority of an excited public opinion deprived him of his office. The storm soon died down, however. Men put their own concerns first: when later the citizens of Europe experienced revolutions still more bloody and extreme, they invariably preferred the safety of their possessions to the prospect of a possible state of anarchy.

Immediately after the event, on December 11, 1851, de

Tocqueville wrote to the editor of *The Times:* "No doubt history will have weighty charges to bring against the Legislative Assembly which has just been illegally and violently dissolved. The parties of which that assembly was composed failed to come to an understanding, and this gave to the whole body an uncertain and sometimes contradictory policy, and finally discredited the assembly and rendered it incapable of defending either liberty or its own existence. History will record this much; but history will reject with contempt the accusation which Louis Napoleon has preferred against us. . . ."[25] We may pass over here the account he gives of the events which led up to the *coup d'état*. He concludes with a terrible indictment of the new regime. "The liberty of the press is destroyed to an extent unheard of even in the time of the empire. . . . Human life is as little respected as human liberty. . . . As for the appeal to the people, to which Louis Napoleon affects to submit his claims, never was a more odious mockery offered to a nation. . . . The people is called upon to express its opinion, but the first measure taken to obtain it is to establish military terrorism throughout the country. . . . Such . . . is the condition in which we stand. Force overturning law, trampling on the liberty of the press and of the person, deriding the popular will, in whose name the Government pretends to act —France torn from the alliance of free nations to be yoked to the despotic monarchies of the Continent—such is the result of this *coup d'état*. If the judgment of the people of England can approve these military saturnalia, and if the facts I have related, and to the accurate truth of which I pledge myself, do not rouse its censures, I shall mourn for you and for ourselves, and for the sacred cause of legal liberty throughout the world; for the public opinion of England is the grand jury of mankind in the cause of freedom, and if its verdict were to acquit the oppressor the oppressed would have no other resource but in God. . . ."[26] His English friends never forgot this profound appeal to the perennial values of the Western world. When he visited London in 1857 to complete his studies for the continuation of his book on the French Revolution, the then first lord of the admiralty put an

English destroyer at his disposal for his return to Cherbourg. This exceptional honor for a former foreign minister of the Second French Republic was, as the English people knew, in reality accorded to the resolute protagonist of European political ideals. De Tocqueville accepted the honor gratefully, but with a characteristic smile at himself.

The letter to *The Times* was Alexis de Tocqueville's last public utterance as a practicing politician. It is full of courage, honor, and profound passion for human freedom. He was very far from glorifying himself by concealing the faults of the Second Republic after the manner of the later democrats of the Weimar Republic. Not one of the ministers whom Adolf Hitler drove out of Germany in 1933 had courage enough to make a similar indictment. De Tocqueville appealed to the eternal norms of history, to the study of which he was now to return. His political career was wrecked, not because he was a failure as a statesman—we have demonstrated the contrary—but because he lacked the hardness and ruthlessness of the political leader, and perhaps also because his high ethical valuation of human dignity and freedom was bound sooner or later to conflict in principle with the categories that direct the modern mass state. The swift decisiveness in action which the practicing politician needs was checked in de Tocqueville by an unalterable inclination to contemplative analysis:

> the native hue of resolution
> is sicklied o'er with the pale cast of thought.

De Tocqueville had, in fact, something of Hamlet in him. A comparison wih Cavour[27] may help to make clear the structural limitations of the Frenchman's political bent. Cavour and de Tocqueville met one another in the London salon of Nassau Senior and the author of *Democracy in America* exercised a deep and abiding influence on the Piedmontese, five years his junior. Cavour adopted the ideas of this book with the ready accessibility of his five and twenty years. "I don't know," he wrote to his brother, "whether I have recommended to you de Tocqueville's

work on America. Royer-Collard calls it a continuation of Montesquieu. Certainly the book is very remarkable and of the most
intense significance for modern times. In my opinion it chiefly
throws light on the political questions of the future. . . ." The
leading political ideas which governed Cavour in his great work
of creating modern Italy may easily be traced to de Tocqueville's
stimulation. The motto, *Libera chiesa in libero stato,* and the
social reforming tendency of Cavour's policy are examples of the
fundamental spiritual community of the two men. Cavour saw
clearly the "providential" character of the democratic process in
the modern European state and society, but he saw equally clearly
that this process was held up by the concentration of the means of
economic power in ever fewer hands, a process which threatened
to hinder the advance of political equality. He thus realized that
the essential for a sound and progressive conduct of affairs in the
modern mass state must aim not only at political freedom, but at
economic reforms in harmony with this end. The Italy of the
risorgimento was the outcome of these views, realized with a re-
lentless severity. "Yet in his heart of hearts," as Croce wrote of
him, "he even loved freedom as much as he detested absolutism."[28] Camillo Cavour effected an unbroken unity of statesmanlike knowledge and political will in a way that was forever
impossible to Alexis de Tocqueville.

The Ancien Régime and the Revolution

De Tocqueville began to write his *Souvenirs* in July 1850, and early in 1851, while still at Sorrento, he carried them down to the close of his period of office as foreign minister. These notes were not primarily intended for publication, and were not in fact published until 1893, when they appeared in incomplete form.* The *Souvenirs* were written principally as a work of self-clarification, though the book must be ranged today among the abiding masterpieces in the literature of political memoirs. "To my sons and grandsons, as an interpretation of the past—as a lesson for the future"—this dictum with which Bismarck later headed his *Reflections and Recollections* might well have served the French statesman as a heading for his *Souvenirs*.

There is no need at this point to give a circumstantial appreciation of the *Souvenirs*. Outstanding passages from the work, affording a lively picture of the political and the social world under the July monarchy and the brief period of the Second French Republic, have been woven into previous chapters of this book. Personalities, the social and political circumstances of the day, and de Tocqueville's own relations to them, are put for the reader with plastic art and with uncompromising self-criticism and subtlety. It may be true to call the *Souvenirs* his finest book: it undoubtedly gives the most immediate expression of his fundamental attitude as a man and a thinker.

The writing of the *Souvenirs* was, nevertheless, a work of

* Cf. now the complete edition which I published in the Meridian Book series, based on the edition published by Gallimard in Paris in 1942.

secondary importance to de Tocqueville at the time. During the
health-giving weeks of that South Italian winter he was concerned
with a greater objective. After more than a decade which in
many respects had proved, as he wrote in a letter to de Kergorlay,
"rather barren,"[1] he wanted to write "a great book." He now
felt more confidence than at the time of the work on America
"in taking in hand a great political book."[2] Should he venture on
a comprehensive portrayal of modern society and of its probable
future? He rejected the plan because of the difficulty of arriving
at a unified conception. "I can see the parts of such a work, but
I cannot see the whole."[3] De Tocqueville, like all great French
thinkers, had a remarkable power of abstraction, yet he was not
as a writer able to work in abstract categories. It was only *through*
history that he could exercise his rare faculty for universal, abstract condensation. "I must find somewhere a solid, lasting basis
of fact for my ideas. I can find this only as I write history—as I
concentrate on an epoch whose story gives me occasion to paint
the men and events of our century, and to build up a unified
picture from all these separate studies. The prolonged drama of
the French Revolution alone furnishes me with these conditions."[4]

It was indeed to be the theme of his last work. The epistolary
passage quoted above is invaluable as an exposition of de Tocqueville's innermost habit of thought. It is from living history alone
that he gets the categories for his interpretation of life. It is a
method of presenting history very far removed from the contemplative and detached vision of Ranke's *Wie es gewesen*. History
is never finished; it lives on in us and directs us, even as we live
on within it, and gives ever fresh form to its effects. Thus there
is no question of a mere record of factual material. "No doubt I
shall indicate the facts," he writes to de Kergorlay, "I shall trace
out their sequence; but my chief business will not be narration. I
must above all make plain the principles, make visible the diverse
causes, which have arisen from it: how the Empire came about;
how it was able to establish itself in the *milieu* of a society created
by the Revolution; what means it employed; what was the *true*
nature of the man who founded it; what made his success and

what his reverses; the passing and the lasting effect he has had upon the destinies of the world, and particularly upon those of France. Here, it seems to me, is material for a very great book. But the difficulties are immense. The one that troubles me most arises from the mingling of history proper with philosophy of history. I do not see yet how I can mix the two things (and it is most important that this should be done, for one can put it that the former is the canvas, the latter the colour—and both these are necessary to make a picture)."[5] A book on which de Tocqueville thought of modeling his work was Montesquieu's *Greatness and Decadence of the Romans*. "One travels without a pause, so to speak," he writes of his great model's method, "across the whole of Roman history, and yet one sees enough of this history to wish for and to understand the author's explanations."[6]

Montesquieu's influence on de Tocqueville can hardly be over-rated. When he wrote his *Democracy in America,* Montesquieu's *Esprit des Lois* was ever-present to him. But Tocqueville was not only deeply familiar with Montesquieu; two other great French magistrates, Bodin and his ancestor Malesherbes, were likewise his guides and examples.

De Tocqueville knew, nevertheless, that his was a harder task than Montesquieu's, because he had to deal with the history of his own times. To see it from a distance comparable to Montesquieu's "one needs to speak of men and things without passion and without reticence. As touching persons, although they have lived in our own times, I am sure of feeling neither love nor hate for them: and as to the forms of things which are called constitutions, laws, dynasties, classes, I can say that for me they have not only no value but no existence independently of the effects they produce. I have no traditions, I have no party, I have above all no *cause* save that of liberty and human dignity. Of this I am certain. . . . "[7] Such were the philosophical and systematic bases from which de Tocqueville approached his new work.

He was, of course, well acquainted with previous histories of the revolution. Thiers's *History of the Revolution* and *History of the Consulate and the Empire,* the books of Mignet, Carlyle, and

Michelet, Louis Blanc's work which had just begun to come out, Lamartine's *Histoire des Girondins,* Madame de Staël's posthumous *Considérations sur les principaux évènements de la Révolution française* (1818)—he had mastered them and passed beyond them.[8] They did no more than clarify for him his own formulation of his subject, for de Tocqueville was no compiler, but an original writer of great stature.

The French Revolution was not a new theme to him, for in 1836, at the request of John Stuart Mill, he published in the *London and Westminster Review* an article entitled "France before the Revolution," in which the most essential theses of *The Ancien Régime and the Revolution* are plainly outlined, while earlier still, in a note to the first volume of *Democracy in America,* are to be found these significant sentences: "It is incorrect to assert that centralization was produced by the French Revolution: the revolution brought it to perfection, but did not create it. The mania for centralization and government regulations dates from the time when jurists began to take a share in the government in the time of Philippe-le-Bel. . . . The fact is that for several centuries past the central power of France has done everything it could to extend central administration; it has acknowledged no other limits than its own strength. The central power to which the Revolution gave birth made more rapid advances than any of its predecessors, because it was stronger and wiser than they had been; Louis XIV committed the welfare of such communities to the caprice of an intendant; Napoleon left them to that of the minister. The same principle governed both. . . ."[9] It is obvious that de Tocqueville had only to work out upon the broad basis of mature personal political experience views which he had held long since.

Despite his shaken health he spent indefatigable months on research into a great variety of Parisian and provincial archives, and during 1855 he applied himself to learning German with the object of studying in Germany certain institutional forms of the medieval social order there, so that he might trace the origins of modern France from their actual sources. This devoted research work is entirely unobtrusive in the completed book, which is provided with comparatively few references. What is today called the apparatus of scholarship (and is often merely a cover for the author's poverty of ideas) was withheld by de Tocqueville from publication, and to this day these papers lie yellowing and unused among the family archives.*

De Tocqueville worked for five years on his new book. It establishes with incontrovertible data and proofs from pre-revolutionary French social history that the centralistic structure of France's administration was in no sense the work of the Revolution—a fact now fully accepted in Western sociology. Never since have the origins of any modern state been presented with an equal precision and clarity.[10] Present-day research into the history of the French Revolution must absolutely agree with de Tocqueville's findings, and this despite the fact that more than eighty years have elapsed since the publication of *The Ancien Régime and the Revolution*. Its author was, indeed, the servant of no party, but only of the truth.

Before discussing the central result of his researches it will be well to outline concisely the work's general conceptual trend. It is divided into three parts, each of which is in its turn lucidly articulated. The first part opens by disposing of certain ideas erroneously accepted at that time. The French Revolution was a political, *not* a religious revolution, notwithstanding that it assumed that quasi-religious character which goes so far to explain its European expansion. "The French Revolution proceeded, in regard to this world, in precisely the same manner that religious revolutions proceed with regard to the next; it looked upon the citizen in the abstract, irrespective of any particular society, just as most religions look upon Man in general independently of time or country. It did not endeavour merely to define what were the especial rights of a French citizen, but what were the universal duties and rights of all men in political matters."[11] The true work

* In the meantime we have edited these papers as volume II, 2 of our edition of Tocqueville's *Œuvres complètes*. My colleague André Jardin has spent many years in putting this material together.

of the Revolution was to annihilate the feudal social order and to replace it by a new political and social order aiming at equality for all citizens. But this process of the annihilation of feudal institutions had actually been in train for centuries.

The second part of the work provides an analysis of the state of administrative and political centralization prevailing under the *ancien régime*. The independent life of the French provinces had long since been extinguished. "Through the diversities which still subsisted, the unity of the nation might already be discerned; uniformity of legislation brought it to light."[12] Their inhabitants, too, were growing more alike. For centuries the French nobility had suffered a process of impoverishment, partly to be accounted for by that progressive subdivision of landed property which to this day gives its peculiar character to the French social structure. "The nobles had sold their lands piecemeal to the peasants, reserving to themselves only the seignorial rights which gave them the appearance rather than the reality of their former position."[13] De Tocqueville established a similar tendency among the German nobility of the Rhine. The English nobility alone knew how not only to maintain but to increase its wealth. "They (the English nobles) were still first in riches as in power. The new families which had risen beside them had copied but had not surpassed their wealth."[14] But in France the one-time riches of the nobility passed into the hands of the bourgeoisie, and toward the close of the eighteenth century differences between the classes above the proletariat lessened noticeably: "they had the same ideas, the same habits, the same tastes; they indulged in the same pleasures, read the same books, and spoke the same language."[15] The only surviving difference was one of formal legal status. Centralization of state administration had been developing for centuries, depriving provinces and cities of their individual freedoms. In this connection de Tocqueville notes that not even ten noblemen might assemble to discuss their common concerns without express permission from the king.

A remnant of freedom persisted only in the corporations, and in the judiciary. A judge could not be deprived of office, and although the absolute power of the king had withdrawn from the proper courts the settlement of almost all cases touching public authority, it had not invariably been able to do so. "Though they [the courts] might be prevented from recording their judgments, the Government did not always dare to prevent them from receiving complaints or from recording their opinions; . . . the magistrates not infrequently stigmatized the acts of the Government as arbitrary and despotic."[16]

In the France of the *ancien régime* there was, accordingly, only an unregulated, one might almost say fortuitous, freedom, whose supporters were nonetheless—or perhaps rather on that account—men proud and bold of spirit. The Revolution took their bearing for its example.

An unjust system of taxation and an almost inextricable tangle of state debts were probably among the most immediate causes of the outbreak of revolution, and Tocqueville analyzes these brilliantly.

In the third part of the work three initial chapters are devoted to examining the role played by political writers, philosophers, and economists in preparing the intellectual climate of the Revolution. It is difficult to summarize these chapters because the threads of the investigation (and this applies to the whole work) are interrupted by reflections of a general kind on the philosophy of history. These chapters in fact contain a sociology of the eighteenth-century French intelligentsia, and those fashionable sociologists of today who hold the modest belief that they have discovered a new scientific discipline would do well to look closely at the method, design, and process of de Tocqueville's investigation, even should the result be diminishing to their pride.

An eighteenth-century French writer was not, like his English colleague of the period, well acquainted with the daily political concerns of his country. The centralized administration excluded him from the realm of practical politics. Yet we can see how French writers, in contrast to German *literati* of the same period who withdrew to the sphere of "pure" philosophy or "pure" art, suddenly turned their attention to questions of *principle* in the social and national order. There ensued an abstract political literature which sought to hold up to the complex world of tradition and custom a new, simple, and elementary conception of society and of the state. Its ideas won ground not only with the bourgeoisie, but even with the aristocracy, for, after all, nothing more was claimed as the sole freedom of the individual under an absolutist regime than freedom to philosophize about the origin of the state, the true nature of government, the rights of man, and allied questions. Men believed that in reason, in enlightenment, they had discovered a tool with which to effect a radical reconstruction of society. Long before the Revolution Louis XVI's own edicts speak of "natural law" and of the basic "rights of man." The ancient world marched unsuspecting toward its doom. What hope could there be of building a new world on empty abstractions when the old world, corrupt and rotten though it might be, had centuries of growth behind it?

The attitude of these new political philosophers was fundamentally antireligious. The Church was deeply involved with the *ancien régime,* and they therefore attacked her also. In this connection de Tocqueville touches upon one of the main axioms of his theory of government. Respect for religion is for him one of the most essential guarantees of a free life within the state. The widespread contempt into which religious dogma had fallen at the end of the eighteenth century gave to the Revolution an antireligious character which was not confined to France, but spread throughout Europe. De Tocqueville indeed notes a measure of reaction. "The old nobility, which was the most irreligious class before 1789, became the most fervent after 1793: it was the first infected, and the first cured. When the bourgeoisie felt itself struck down in its triumph, it began also, in its turn, gradually to revert to religious faith."[17]

There is no doubt that this is historically correct, but it is questionable whether the cautious generalization which sees in this reaction toward religion a fundamental tendency of the last "sixty years" can be maintained today. The process of secularization of Western society, in which the eighteenth century marked so important a stage with its doctrine of human perfectibility and social progress, continues to exercise its leveling effect unchecked down to the present day if we leave out of account certain solitary and uninfluential voices which are lifted here and there. This process of secularization is certainly antireligious, as de Tocqueville, Jansenistically-minded and an admirer of Pascal, affirmed; but, if we read the signs of the future aright, it tends to be final.

There will continue to be individual mystics, such as Rainer Maria Rilke, in the great cities of Europe, and simple believers in the old sense in the villages, except where these are delivered, helpless victims, through political parties, the cinema, and radio and television, to other norms of belief. Yet the irreligious world of the twentieth century is a visible fact. Alexis de Tocqueville may have had a presentiment of it, though his political philosophy halts at this frontier. There will be occasion to consider this later.

De Tocqueville's sociology of the eighteenth-century French intelligentsia as treated in the chapters under consideration did not confine itself, like our fashionable sociology today, to an exposition of special class relationships and the sociological significance of the contrasts they present in some given social situation, but rather comprised in its analysis the norm of a definite political and philosophical attitude of the kind that our contemporary sociology poor-spiritedly rejects under the plea of scientific objectivity. The fact, its interpretation, and a deliberate political standpoint are inseparable—such is the very meaning of the philosophical approach to history, and such is the lesson which may be learned again and again in reading *The Ancien Régime and the Revolution*.

In a later chapter of the third part of his work de Tocqueville shows how "the reign of Louis XVI was the most flourishing period of the ancient monarchy, and how its very prosperity hastened the Revolution." In this connection, however, later research[18] in economic history has shown that in 1789, as a result of bad harvests, the highest price was paid for cereals in France since 1734, and that furthermore a grave industrial crisis, due to superior technical equipment of the English factories over the

French, led to widespread unemployment. In regard to the economic causes of the Revolution these facts call for a considerable modification of de Tocqueville's account of things, but he formulated, nonetheless, a thesis which reveals deep insight into the revolutionary mechanism. "The state of things destroyed by a revolution," he wrote, "is almost always somewhat better than that which immediately preceded it; and experience has shown that the most dangerous moment for a bad government is usually that when it enters upon the work of reform."[19] Although in 1789 private wealth and state wealth were greatly entangled, the most determined advocates of radical financial reform were the owners of private capital, though of course "without reflecting that to touch this part of the Government was to cause every other part to fall."[20]

Revolution was inevitable. "On the one hand, a nation in which the appetite for making fortunes extended every day—on the other, a Government which incessantly excited this passion, which agitated, inflamed, and beggared the nation, driving by either path towards its own destruction."[21]

In a brilliant closing chapter de Tocqueville gives a résumé of his investigations of the old France and the new. Let us set forth its outstanding points:

(*a*) Despite the loss of their ancient political rights the French aristocracy had retained privileges which isolated them within the nation as a detested caste.

(*b*) The absolutist regime had abolished the freedom of the provinces, and made itself master of the administration, so that Paris became France.

(*c*) The bourgeoisie had become unaccustomed to any and every kind of concern with political matters.

(*d*) The philosophers became representative of public opinion: "It might be anticipated that instead of endeavouring separately to amend the laws which were bad, all laws would be attacked, and that an attempt would be made to substitute for the ancient constitution of France an entirely novel system of government, conceived by these writers."[22]

(*e*) The Catholic Church was closely bound up with the *ancien régime*.

(*f*) As to the contrast between the humanitarianism of theory and the brutality of practice during the Revolution "books had supplied the theory; the people undertook its practical application, and adapted the conceptions of these writers to the impulse of their own actions."[23]

(*g*) There was a passion for equality and freedom. Of the latter de Tocqueville remarks that it was "the more recent" and "less firmly rooted" of the two.[24] On their co-ordination in the first enthusiasm of the Revolution he says: "Then, indeed, the French were sufficiently proud of their cause and of themselves to believe that they might be equal in freedom."[25]

(*h*) Freedom turned to despotism: Napoleon. "But when that vigorous generation, which had conceived the Revolution was destroyed or enervated, as commonly happens to any generation which engages in such enterprises—when, following the natural course of events of this nature, the love of freedom had been dampened and discouraged by anarchy and popular tyranny, and the bewildered nation began to grope after a master, absolute government found prodigious facilities for recovering and consolidating its authority, and these were easily discovered by the genius of the man who was to continue the Revolution and to destroy it."[26]

At the end of his book de Tocqueville assures his reader that he has led him only to the threshold of the Revolution, yet the concise characterization indicated in the foregoing summary sketches the whole course of the revolutionary movement from the summoning of the States General in 1789 up to the establishment of Napoleon's plebiscitary democracy.

The work was indeed a great achievement, and its reception was not less enthusiastic than that accorded twenty years earlier to the book on America. *The Ancien Régime and the Revolution* is one of the rare European books which accompany history with a philosophic commentary. Others are Montesquieu's *Considérations sur les causes de la grandeur des Romains et de leur décadence,* Vico's *Scienza nuova,* made available to French readers by Michelet twenty years earlier. Hegel's *Vorlesungen über die Philosophie der Weltgeschichte,* Jacob Burckhardt's *Weltgeschichtliche Betrachtungen,* and certain posthumous volumes by Lord Acton. De Tocqueville's *Souvenirs* no doubt give the most direct impression of his personality, but in my view his book on the ancient France and the new is his most important work. The style and the articulation of ideas show an incomparable precision: with controlled and practiced hand the master hews out a monumental contribution to political thought which will retain its validity as long as there are Europeans who seek to understand the meaning of their history.

Among the *Œuvres complètes* there are a number of fragments which show in outline plans for the continuation of the work, and in unpublished papers* in the archives of the de Tocqueville family there are also studies of Lafayette, Barnave, etc.; but de Tocqueville was destined never to shape these fragments to formal unity. His strength failed, and his death in 1859 put an end to his grand project for carrying his readers across the threshold of the Revolution.

It must on no account be forgotten, however, that the completed first volume needs some conception of the work *as a whole* for its proper estimation. De Tocqueville's aim was always that of the "retrospective prophet" as in Friedrich Schlegel's very happy definition of the historian's task. There are many passages in *The Ancien Régime and the Revolution* which indicate how the lines of the exposition were to be carried on into the fifties of the nineteenth century. De Tocqueville meant also to interpret his own times.

Among the posthumously published papers there is a fragment (written at Sorrento in December 1850) which throws light on the close association of de Tocqueville's work with contemporary affairs. This fragment deals with Napoleon I, and its most es-

* Cf. now volume II, 2 of my edition of Alexis de Tocqueville's complete works, where these papers have been made available, admirably edited by my colleague André Jardin.

sential passages may be quoted here: "What I want to portray is less the facts themselves—surprising and significant as these are—than the spirit of the facts: less the different acts of Napoleon's career than Napoleon himself—that strange, that incomplete yet marvelous man to contemplate whom is to become a spectator of one of the strangest phenomena this universe affords.

"I want to show what in his prodigious enterprises he really drew from his genius, and what from the facilities afforded him by the state of the country and the spirit of the times; to show how and why this intractable nation rushed, as it were, at that moment, of its own impulse into slavery, and with what incomparable art this man discovered in creations of the most demagogic of revolutions everything that favoured despotism—and drew it out.

"As regards his domestic policy I want to observe how this almost divine intelligence was employed on the brutal task of curtailing human liberty; to watch an intelligent and perfected organization of force such as could have been conceived only by the greatest of geniuses in the most enlightened and civilized of centuries; and to see how society, cramped and suffocated under the weight of this admirable machine, grew sterile; how intellectual activity slackened, the human spirit grew languid, souls grew narrow, great men ceased to appear, and there remained a vast level horizon where, turn as one might, nothing was to be seen but the colossal figure of the Emperor himself.

"Coming to his foreign policy and his conquests, I shall seek to depict the whirlwind of his career, sweeping over peoples and kingdoms; I want to explain how here too the strange splendour of his genius for war was assisted by the strange grandeur and disorder of the times. What an amazing picture, if one could but paint it, of human power and human weakness in this impatient, mutable genius, continually making and unmaking his own works, himself pulling down and replacing the frontiers of empires, and driving nations and rulers desperate less by what he made them suffer than by the everlasting uncertainty he imposed on them as to what they might have to fear in the future!

"I want finally to make clear by what course of excesses and errors he precipitated his own fall: to trace, despite these errors and excesses, the tremendous mark he has left upon the world, not only as a memory but in durable influence and actions—what died with him and what survives.

"To complete the big canvas I want to show the significance of the Empire in the French Revolution—the true place of this strange act in a strange play, the *dénouement of which escapes us yet.*"[27] These last words (the italics are ours) throw light on the exemplary conceptions which de Tocqueville associated with the first stage of the French Revolution. Had he not already (as indicated above) described the political and social movements of his own day simply as a continuation of this first revolutionary phase? What was the *nature* of this great revolutionary movement which began at the close of the eighteenth century, which profoundly changed nineteenth-century social order, and whose tide flows to this very day, even while we seek to revivify the figure of this great French social philosopher?

The *political* tendency of the first revolutionary phase, which de Tocqueville is inclined to assign to the years 1789 to 1848, is followed in 1848 by a *social* phase which, as he rightly sees, questions the very basis of bourgeois society as such. But he observed this social revolution only as a tendency, as a beginning. There are many passages in his writings and letters in which he tries to describe the purport of this new social-revolutionary tendency in Europe. For example, he writes in a letter to Stoffels, on April 28, 1850: "It is clear to me that people have been mistaken these last sixty years in thinking the revolution to be *over*. They thought the revolution was finished on the 18th Brumaire; they thought it was finished in 1814; I thought myself in 1830 that it was finished indeed when democracy had destroyed all privileges save the very old and very necessary one of property. I thought that, like the ocean, the revolution had at last found a shore. It was a mistake. It is plain to-day that the tide continues to flow, that the waters still rise, that not only have we not seen the end of the vast revolution which began before our time, but that even the infant born to-day will probably never see it. *It is a matter not of the modification but of the transformation of the social body.* [The italics are ours.] What is the goal? Indeed, I don't know, and I believe it is beyond the intelligence of any of us. One feels that the old world is coming to an end. What will the new be like? The greatest minds of the time are no more able to tell than were those of antiquity able to foresee the abolition of slavery, a Christian society, the barbarian invasion, and all the other great events which renewed the face of the earth. They felt simply that the social order of their day was in dissolution, that was all. . . .To come to a matter more precise and less remote I do not think that French society as it is to-day is as closely threatened as people fear. It still contains infinitely too much vital force to allow itself to perish. . . ."[28] Ideas similar to those in the letter just quoted occupied de Tocqueville in the *Souvenirs,* where he writes: "And behold the French Revolution beginning again, for it is indeed the same! As the years pass it lengthens out, and the end is hidden from us. Shall we attain, as some prophets, perhaps as vain as their predecessors, assure us, a social transformation more complete and more profound than our fathers foresaw or desired, than we ourselves are able to foresee? *Or are we about to enter on intermittent anarchy—that chronic and incurable malady, well-known to ancient peoples?* [The italics are ours.] For myself, I cannot say, I do not know when the long journey will end. I'm tired of again and again mistaking misleading cloud-banks for the shore, and I often ask myself whether the *terra firma* we have sought so long really exists and whether it is not our destiny to contend with the ocean for ever!"[29]

De Tocqueville's clear vision of imminent revolutionary changes in Western social order is apparent, yet he could not penetrate the mists of the future even though, all the while, in the almost contemporaneous works of Karl Marx, material already existed which might have given him a clearer perception of the future social structure of the Western world. He believed a socialistic order which questioned the justification of private ownership of the means of production to be impossible of accomplishment. At this point probably lay the actual limit of his political conceptions. And yet any future reconstitution of social order in the European states is conceivable only on the basis of some new conception of "rights of ownership." By 1850 Marx himself had clarified those ideas on the difference in principle between individual property and social ownership of the means of production, later to be expressed in *Das Kapital,* for in his *Eighteenth Brumaire,* which was of the same date as the document quoted above, he writes: "The social revolution of the nineteenth century cannot draw its figurative embellishments from the past; it must create them anew out of the future. It cannot begin its work until it has got rid itself of all the ancient superstitions. Earlier revolutions had need of the reminiscences of historic pageantry, for thus only could they delude themselves as to their own significance. The revolution of the nineteenth century [and we may add today—1939—also the revolution of the twentieth century] must let the dead bury their dead, for only thus can it discover its own true meaning. In those earlier revolutions, there was more phrase than substance; in the revolution that is to come, there will be more substance than phrase."[30]

Marx later attempted a closer definition of the content of this new revolution which, indeed, in 1851, showed "more substance than phrase." I do not attribute permanent value to his attempt, yet I can conceive no positive and constructive plan for a new social order which could afford to ignore Marx's conclusions.

We have dealt with the question of how de Tocqueville ordered the '48 movement in the march of world events under the banner of the *one* Revolution. Now it will be necessary to show even more pointedly de Tocqueville's place in the framework of his epoch. He suffered unspeakably from the mediocrity of his age, whose representatives were the French middle classes (*la bourgeoisie moyenne*). He characterized their spirit, as may be remembered, with cutting acumen in the early pages of the *Souvenirs.* "It was an orderly, industrious, often dishonest spirit, often full of vanity and egotism, bold yet temperamentally timid, moderate in all things except the love of easy living—in a word, *mediocre*." This spirit was no longer confined to the two hundred thousand privileged citizens who constituted Guizot's *pays légal*, but possessed the millions who hailed in Louis Napoleon, in de Tocqueville's own pointed epigram, "crude mediocrity." This *enrichissez-vous* spirit has been preserved to futurity in Daumier's caricatures and on every page of Flaubert's great novel, *L'Éducation sentimentale*.

The French middle class of 1848 wanted to see their citizen rights assured as against the hitherto privileged enfranchised group of two hundred thousand, and to that extent they represented the interests of the young French proletarian movement; but no sooner were these rights assured to them than this same middle class, now making common cause with the upper bourgeoisie, opposed any claim on the part of the proletariat which might prejudice their profits and securities. Bourgeois rights of property might on no account be called in question. The French bourgeois was the only true victor in the great conflict of the French Revolution.

In a passage in his *Souvenirs* de Tocqueville says that the revolutionary movement of 1848 was in his view a mere game in comparison with that of 1789—an idea more pointedly expressed by Marx in his *Eighteenth Brumaire* by the twist he gives to a dictum of Hegel to the effect that all historical events happen twice over, the first time as tragedy, the second as comedy. Writing in 1939 I am inclined to add that they happen three times—the third time as farce!

The aims of the 1789 movement were genuinely humanitarian and idealistic, but the outcome of all that immense enthusiasm was a compromise between the material and spiritual interests of the French bourgeoisie; the dreams of eighteenth-century philosophers were relegated to the archives: the good burgher could now sleep peacefully in his bed.

In 1848 a wider and broader bourgeois group forced its way into the territory of a hitherto privileged upper middle class, and if this new group appealed to the ideals of the Girondists or

Montagnards it was but in pretense; in reality it only wanted to enjoy bourgeois security and to make safe profits.

The " '48," disguised as a great historic movement did indeed make comedy of tragedy: with Caussidière in the role of Danton, Louis Blanc as Robespierre, and Louis Napoleon as Napoleon Bonaparte there was matter enough for laughter! And now we in these days have reached farce—a farce performed by the Fascist and National Socialist movements! Once again large new groups have shouldered their way into the old bourgeois ranks—the *ceti medi* of Italy and the *Mittelschichten* of Germany. They *alone* represent the new masses of the Fascist states, and in Hitler and Mussolini they have found men who speak their speech, the language of mediocrity, the only one they can understand. This triple process, from tragedy to comedy, and again from comedy to farce, is indeed one way of describing the far-reaching movement which entered the theater of Western history in 1789.[30a]

In *The Ancien Régime and the Revolution* de Tocqueville attempted to establish the position of his own epoch in the wider pattern of French social history. We may remember his letter to the editor of *The Times,* in which he expressed distinctly and unmistakably his loathing for the regime of Louis Napoleon. His private correspondence after 1851 (of which Antoine Redier has made public a few hitherto unpublished letters) shows with what painful feelings he watched the fate of France under the Second Empire.

In a letter of February 1852 he bitterly reproaches his brother, who had given implicit recognition to the new regime. "It is not a question, it is said, of supporting Louis Napoleon, but of upholding authority, morality, religion. This is philosophers' talk, my dear brother, not the talk of politicians. It is a matter not of what one would wish, but of what one is to do.

"Besides, can you believe for a moment that to employ the means that have been employed and to do what has been done will re-establish *authority?* . . . Do you not see . . . that he is establishing an extreme order of things which inevitably challenges the opposite extreme? . . .

"Do you believe that one can re-establish morality by giving the world the most glaring example in all history of trickery, violence, and perjury triumphing in the acclamations wrested by fear from a section of the educated and respectable classes? Do you think that tottering morality can be re-established by an example of the violation of all laws, by the sight of the country's best men in prison vans, the greatest generals of the day treated like convicts or banished as public enemies simply for the crime of having been faithful to their commissions and to the laws of their country? . . .

"And as to religion, consider this and remember it one day: up to the present, God be thanked, only a section of the clergy have subscribed to this *régime*. But if, unhappily, there should be a public impression that the whole clergy have espoused this cause, there could be no more terrible blow to religion in this country. . . ."[31]

It is almost surprising that these sentences were written in 1852 and not in 1922 or 1933!

De Tocqueville was very far from denying the fresh impetus to French business which the Second Empire brought with it. "Business," he writes in a letter dated the end of November 1853, "has a feverish character. The transactions on the Bourse can only be compared to those of Law's time. Public undertakings are multiplied in an extravagant manner. . . . Well, despite all that, unless the Government makes huge mistakes, it will last long enough, and no one is in a position to say how it will end and what will replace it."[32]

Scarcely two months later, however, he got a clearer view on this point also. "War alone can bring him [Louis Napoleon] to quick destruction, and war will destroy us all with him."[33] No illusions could dim the penetrating insight of the great political analyst.

In a very important document of the same year de Tocqueville expounds, for the benefit of the Comte de Chambord, legitimist Bourbon pretender, certain points needing to be clearly envisaged by any future government of France. Louis Napoleon's regime, he says in this memorandum (first published by Antoine Redier), will either persist or it will be destroyed by the spirit of freedom. The spirit of freedom, in de Tocqueville's estimation, can only be maintained by a strong constitutional monarchy guaranteeing personal liberty; by a true, national representation of the people assuring the freedom and complete publicity of parliamentary debate; and, finally, by the freedom of a *genuine* press (*presse réelle*). Further remarks make it plain that he envisaged this freedom as being administered only in carefully measured doses; for otherwise there would be a danger of renewing the anarchy of the Second Republic.

I do not think that de Tocqueville saw the re-establishment of a constitutional Bourbon monarchy as more than a vague political possibility, and I have therefore confined myself to a mere summary mention of the exposé designed for the Comte de Chambord. It is, indeed, a matter of common experience that during the early years of a dictatorial government the politically minded tend to buoy themselves up with hopes of a speedy overthrow of the regime they detest.

The preface to *The Ancien Régime and the Revolution* formulates the substance of de Tocqueville's political conceptions, with plain reference to Napoleon III's plebiscitary dictatorship. "Amidst the darkness of the future three truths may be clearly discovered. The first is, that all the men of our time are impelled by an unknown force which they may hope to regulate and to check, but not to conquer—a force which sometimes gently moves them, sometimes hurries them along, to the destruction of aristocracy. The second is, that of all the societies in the world those which will always be least able permanently to escape from absolute government are precisely the societies in which aristocracy has ceased to exist and can never exist again. The third and last is, that despotism nowhere produces more pernicious effects than in these same societies, for more than any other form of government, despotism favours the growth of all the vices to which such societies are specially liable, and thus throws an additional weight on that side to which, by their natural inclination, they are already prone.

"Men in such countries, being no longer connected together by any ties of caste, class, corporation, or family, are but too easily inclined to think of nothing but their private interests, ever too ready to consider themselves only, and to sink into the narrow precincts of self, in which all public virtue is extinguished. Despotism, instead of combating this tendency, renders it irresistible, for it deprives its subjects of every common passion, of every mutual want, of all necessity of combining together, of all occasions of acting together. It immures them in private life. . . ."[34] "Freedom alone," continues de Tocqueville in another paragraph, "can effectually counteract in societies of this kind the vices which are natural to them, and restrain them on the declivity down which they glide. For freedom alone can withdraw the members of such a society from the isolation in which the very dependence of their condition places them by compelling them to act together. Freedom alone can warm and unite them day by day through the necessity for mutual agreement, for mutual persuasion, and mutual complaisance in the transaction of their common affairs. . . ."[35]

A careful distinction should therefore be made between free and unfree democratic societies—a distinction of which our own day stands in need of reminder. On this point, too, the preface to *The Ancien Régime and the Revolution* is revealing. "Democratic societies which are not free may be rich, refined, adorned, magnificent, powerful by the weight of their uniform mass; they may contain many private merits, good fathers of families, honest traders, estimable men of property; nay, many good Christians will be found there, for their country is not of this world, and the glory of their faith is to produce such men from the midst of the greatest depravity of manners and under the worst government. The Roman empire in its extreme decay was full of such men. But that which, I am confident, will never be found in such societies, is a great citizen, or, above all, a great people; nay, I do not hesitate to affirm *that the common level of the heart and intellect will never cease to sink as long as equality of conditions and despotic power are combined there.*[36] (The italics are ours.) If these brilliant theses are complemented by those exact conceptions of a regulated and balanced freedom expressed in de Tocqueville's work on America and in the notes designed for the Bourbon pretender of 1853, the fundamental structural lines of de Tocqueville's doctrine of the state and of society will be apparent. He teaches not only that there may be both free and unfree democracies, but that there are two kinds of freedom—the freedom of caprice and that other freedom which is governed by the eternal laws of human dignity and human morality. In his own words: "Despots themselves do not deny the excellence of freedom, but they wish to keep it all to themselves, and maintain that all other men are utterly unworthy of it. Thus it is not in the opinion which may be entertained of freedom that this difference subsists, but in the greater or the less esteem we may have for mankind."[37]

De Tocqueville's last great work was finished. When *The Ancien Régime and the Revolution* was published he was fifty-one years old, and he had but three more years to live. Dark shadows lay over his beloved France, the false glitter of the Second Empire notwithstanding. But his faith in the light of human freedom and human dignity was unshakable. For him these things were as everlasting as the stars.

SEVEN

Political Philosophy

In the earlier pages of this study we have shown that from his first youth de Tocqueville was ambitious to serve his country as a politician. But had he the special ability—the doubt appears again and again in the intimate letters of his earlier years—to become a political leader in France? De Tocqueville became foreign minister because he wanted political power. The lust for power is, according to Hobbes, the fundamental urge of the political man, and de Tocqueville was undoubtedly possessed by this urge, but in him the power impulse was restrained by a profound social consciousness: he was incapable of wanting power simply for power's sake.

De Tocqueville was no disciple of Machiavelli, and had rejected with all his soul the great Florentine's political pragmatism. "The Machiavelli of *The History of Florence* is to me the Machiavelli of *The Prince*. . . . In his *History* Machiavelli sometimes praises great and noble actions, but you can see that for him it is a matter of the imagination. Fundamentally, he thinks that all actions are indifferent in themselves, and that they must be judged by the skill they display and by the success which follows them. *For him the world is a grand arena, whence God is absent, where conscience has no place, and where every one must fight as best he can for his own end.*"[1] (The italics are ours.) He held that politics without a humanitarian conscience were inhuman and godless.

Statesmanship means more than the technical knowledge and

ability to regulate the life of the community within the state; it involves rather the interadjustment of man's manifold capacities to form a unity both in knowledge and in practice. Feelings, instincts, passions, religion, morality, art, and philosophy are all ingredients in the juristic, administrative, and national institutions of human societies, and the science of statecraft must attempt to analyze this complicated unity and to bring to light its basic elements.

At the annual public meeting of the Académie des Sciences Morales et Politiques of April 2, 1853, de Tocqueville made a speech in which he undertook to define political science. "In politics there are two aspects which ought on no account to be confounded—the one fixed and the other elastic.

"The first is founded in the very nature of man, of his interests, his faculties, the needs revealed by philosophy and history, the instincts which change their objects with the times, *but never change their nature, and are as immortal as the race itself* [the italics are ours]. It is this aspect, I say, that teaches us what laws are most appropriate for the general and permanent condition of humanity. All this is a matter of science.

"But there is also a practical and militant aspect of politics which wrestles with the difficulties of the day as they arise, changes with changing incidents, provides for the passing needs of the moment, and makes use of the ephemeral passions of the age. This is the art of government.

"Undoubtedly there is a difference between the art and the science; practice often diverges from theory—I do not deny it. I will go further, if you like, and concede that to excel in the one is no reason for being successful in the other. . . .

"The art of writing does, in fact, give to those who have long practised it habits of mind unfavourable to the conduct of affairs. It makes them subject to the logic of ideas, whereas the mass obeys only that of its passions. It gives a taste for what is delicate, fine, ingenious, and original, whereas the veriest commonplaces rule the world.

"The study of history itself, while it often throws light on present facts, may sometimes obscure them. How many there are among us who, with their heads enveloped in thick clouds of learning, saw 1640 in 1789 and 1688 in 1830, and who, always one revolution behind the times, tried to apply to the second the treatment appropriate to the first. . . ."[2]

I know of no modern politician who has more deeply illumined the relationship between theory and practice in politics. The differing logics which underlie political thought and political action are sharply defined, and we are reminded, even to the actual words used, of Pascal's distinction between *ordre logique* and *ordre du cœur*. De Tocqueville also points clearly to the dangers of knowing too much about history (so brilliantly castigated twenty years later by Nietzsche in his *Zweite Unzeitgemässe Betrachtung*), though he does not question the "uses of history" within certain limits.

After clearly distinguishing it from the art of government, de Tocqueville proceeds to delineate politics as a pure science. "The science that treats of the guidance of societies covers, indeed, a very wide field which extends from philosophy to the elementary study of civil law. Its field, in fact, is so nearly boundless that it becomes a somewhat indefinite object of vision. It becomes confused with all the branches of learning which relate directly or indirectly to Man, and in this vast area is lost to view.

"Yet when one concentrates one's attention on this great science, setting aside all that adjoins but does not belong to it, the divers parts which compose it do actually appear and one gains at last a clear idea of the whole. One can trace its descent by regular degrees from the general to the particular, from pure theory to written statutes and facts."[3] He then goes on to distinguish four grades or groups which together constitute political philosophy: (1) The universal philosophy of government, as whose greatest writers and teachers he cites Plato, Aristotle, Machiavelli, Montesquieu, and Rousseau. (2) The law of nations, represented by Grotius and Pufendorf. (3) Special branches of statecraft (without touching the general and theoretical character of political philosophy) such, for example, as

General Criminal Law (Beccaria) and Political Economy (Adam Smith). (4) Jurisprudence and juristic commentaries "which explain and interpret existing institutions, covenants, constitutions, and laws." There is, in effect, a descent from the realm of ideas to the facts in which the unity of political philosophy has its roots.

It is natural enough that de Tocqueville (then engaged on his work on the Revolution) should illustrate his exposition of political science by the influence exercised by political writers of the eighteenth century on the French Revolution; necessary comment on this point has been made earlier in this book. Thence he embarks on a general characterization of the function of political science in social life. "And note too that what the political sciences achieved there (i.e. in the Revolution) with such irresistible force and brilliance they achieve everywhere and always, though more secretly and more slowly. *Among all civilized peoples the political sciences give birth or at least form to those general concepts* [the italics are ours] whence emerge the facts with which politicians have to deal, and the laws of which they believe themselves the inventors. They form a kind of atmosphere surrounding each society in which both rulers and governed have to draw intellectual breath, and whence—often without realizing it—both groups derive the principles of action. Only among barbarians does the practical side of politics exist alone."[4] Thus the political rulers of the Greek city states took counsel from Aristotle, Cicero formulated Roman republican ideas of the state, and Thomas Aquinas those of medievalism in his *De regimine principum;* Machiavelli gave theoretical expression to sixteenth-century absolutism; Locke to the political achievements of the English bourgeoisie of 1689; while de Tocqueville's own task was to be the first thinker to lay down the principles of the era of mass democracy. Later Georges Sorel, Max Weber, and Graham Wallas (to name only the most outstanding) were to follow him, but he holds forever the honors of the pioneer.

In the main, indeed, his solitary voice of admonition has found little echo, for this mass era cannot follow the subtle analyses of such a mind as de Tocqueville's, and is, moreover, too self-confident in achievement to suffer criticism. I have written earlier of de Tocqueville's profound sense of isolation among his own contemporaries—a feeling which increased upon him under the dictatorship of Napoleon III. "I regard liberty, as I have always done, as the first of blessings; I see in it one of the most fruitful sources of manly virtue and great actions. I would never surrender it for tranquillity or well-being. Yet I see that most of my contemporaries—I speak of the best of them, for I care little what the others feel—endeavour to accommodate themselves as well as possible to a very different *régime,* and—what troubles and indeed horrifies my soul—would appear to make a readiness for servitude a part of virtue! I could not so think and feel even if I would. My nature revolts from it even more than my will. An indomitable instinct constrains me to be as I have always been on this point."[5] This loneliness of the individual who refuses to surrender hope and belief in freedom in this our age of modern mass dictatorship is indeed agonizing. "I have no child to be pleased by my small share of fame; I scarcely believe that writings such as mine could have the least influence in such times as these—nor indeed any writings except perhaps the bad novels which may have the undesirable effect of making us even more demoralized and disorderly than we are already."[6] It is almost exactly eighty years since de Tocqueville wrote this sentence. He would not have changed a word today. The greatness of his political philosophy appears not least in his perseverance with his work, despite his insight.

He was not one of those intellectuals who enjoy making play with constructive yet empty abstractions. He was no modern professor of philosophy, and would probably have found little acceptance with one. Faguet notes a passage in which de Tocqueville analyzes the principles of his own philosophy of history, and at the same time shows plainly enough how foreign to his thought was empty theorization. "I have lived amongst men of letters who have written history without mixing in affairs, and amongst politicians who have been occupied with making things happen without ever troubling to write about them. I have always noticed that the former see general causes on all sides, while the latter, living in the haphazard of daily events, prefer to think that everything that happens must be attributed to particular accidents and that their petty daily string-pulling represents the forces that move the world. I believe that both are mistaken. For my part I hate these absolute systems which make all the events of history depend on great first causes by a chain of fatality, and which, as it were, exclude man from the history of mankind. . . . I believe, with all due deference to the writers who have invented these sublime theories to nourish their vanity and facilitate their work, that many important historical facts can only be accounted for by accidental circumstances, and that many others remain inexplicable, and that, in fine, chance, or rather that network of secondary causes which we call chance since we are unable to unravel it, counts for much in all that we see in the theatre of this world. . . . Antecedent facts, the nature of institutions, mental attitudes, the state of morals—these are the materials from which are composed those *impromptus* which amaze and terrify us."[7] De Tocqueville was a political philosopher in the true sense, for he sought for the principles of man's political activities tirelessly and with persistent curiosity.

The riddle of man's nature is the starting point of all political philosophy, for all that our modern shallow and short-sighted political thinking, so often blind to all but immediate aims, seems quite to have forgotten this dimension of politics. Again and again de Tocqueville's thought penetrates to this fundamental aspect of political philosophy. In a masterly passage in one of his letters (he was a great letter writer) he defines his own method of thinking as against traditional philosophic thought. "I should have had a passion for those philosophical studies which you have been engaged on all your life if I had been able to get more profit from them, but, whether be it a defect of my mind, or lack of courage in pursuit of my plans, or the special character of the material, I have always reached a point at which I have found that the notions given me by these sciences get me no further—indeed not so far—as I could reach at once by means of just a few quite simple ideas shared more or less by all men. *These ideas easily lead to belief in a first cause which is at once evident and inconceivable: to fixed laws, apparent in the physical world and a necessary supposition in the moral world: to God's providence, and, consequently, His justice:* to man's responsibility for his actions, since he is permitted to know good and evil, and, consequently, to *belief in a future life* [the italics are ours]. I confess to you that, outside revelation, I have never found that the most subtle metaphysic could give me clearer notions on these points than the plainest commonsense, and that has given me rather a grudge against it! What I have called *the bottom which I am unable to* touch is the *wherefore* of the world—the plan of this creation of which we know nothing, not even our bodies and still less our spirits—the reason of the destiny of that singular being whom we call Man, to whom has been given just light enough to show him the miseries of his condition, but not enough to change them. . . ."[8] In these sentences de Tocqueville develops his philosophical creed—a creed in which the frontiers of the knowable are fixed with a calm and a reverence reminiscent of Goethe's wisdom. Two further excerpts bearing on the same subject may be added here to round off the passage just quoted. In a letter of August 5, 1836, to Count Kergorlay we read: "Do what you will you can't change the fact that men have bodies as well as souls—that the angel is enclosed in the beast. . . . Any philosophy, any religion, which tries to leave entirely out of account one of these two things may produce a few extraordinary examples, but will never influence humanity as a whole. This is what I believe, and it troubles me, for you know that, though no more detached than any other from the beast, I adore the angel and want at all costs to see him predominate. I rack my brains unceasingly to discover if there is not some middle way for humanity between these two extremes, leading neither to Heliogabalus nor St. Jerome: for I feel assured that no one will ever draw the majority of men either to the one or the other, and even less to the second than to the first."[9] Man is a mixture of good and evil forces.

The third passage—one of great importance for the understanding of de Tocqueville's fundamental anthropological conceptions—occurs in a letter of January 3, 1843, to Eugène Stoffels. "Men in general are neither very good nor very bad, but mediocre. . . . Man with his vices, his weaknesses, his virtues, this confused medley of good and ill, high and low, goodness and depravity, is yet, take him all in all, the object on earth most worthy of study, of interest, of pity, of attachment, and of admiration. And since we haven't got angels, we can attach ourselves to nothing greater and more worthy of our devotion than our own kind."[10] De Tocqueville, like Plato, envisaged man as an intermediate being, but he never doubted the divine character in the human creature. He had nothing but disgust and scorn for a racial interpretation of human nature, such as that propounded by his friend Count Gobineau. This is apparent when he writes to an English friend that: "Here on the continent books are continually appearing which have for aim—or may have for effect —the restriction or the annihilation of the idea of liberty. The Germans notably are doing their very best to prove that men are like horses, and that it is enough to substitute one strain of blood for another to give them different feelings and different ideas. There has recently appeared in France a big book in four volumes which imparts these fine discoveries."[11] The reference is to Gobineau's book, *The Inequality of Human Races,* which, as is well known, through H. S. Chamberlain exercised a strong influence on German National Socialism. In his correspondence with Gobineau himself there is to be found a detailed critical analysis of the race theory, which is one of the finest and best ever written upon a problem which is rampant in present-day Europe, and which is in reality a question based on false premises.[12]

This conception of humanity runs through all de Tocqueville's thinking on the relations between the state and society as expressed in the books of which we have treated in the foregoing chapters. His thinking, as we have seen, shows none of the marks of abstract utopianism. De Tocqueville traces out the underlying structures of the historical process in the Western world from the Middle Ages onward in a spirit of absolute loyalty to historical and sociological realities as he sees them. It appeared to him inevitable that aristocracy would disappear, drowned under the advancing tides of the democratic masses. The new democratic states, however, are not forms of society in which freedom and equality must necessarily flourish together. The great danger of developing democracy lay in the fact that it favored equality but suppressed freedom. Thus to de Tocqueville freedom and democracy were by no means identical.

But how did he define the nature of freedom—a question that must indeed be asked if we are to distinguish a truly free form of democracy from its possible opposite or distortion? De Tocqueville does not fail to give us an answer. He gives it with unsurpassable penetration in his *Ancien Régime and the Revolution:* "I have often asked myself what is the source of that passion for political freedom which in all ages has been the fruitful mother of the greatest things which mankind has achieved—and in what feelings that passion strikes root and finds its nourishment.

"It is evident that when nations are ill-directed they readily conceive the wish to govern themselves; but a love of independence which only springs up under the influence of certain transient evils produced by despotism, is never lasting: it passes away with the accident that gave rise to it; and what seemed to be the love of freedom was no more than the hatred of a master. That which nations made to be free really hate is the curse of dependence.

"Nor do I believe that the true love of freedom is ever born of the mere aspect of its material advantages; for this aspect may frequently happen to be overcast. It is very true that in the long run freedom ever brings to those who know how to keep it, ease, comfort, and often wealth; but there are times at which it disturbs for a season the possession of these blessings; there are other times when despotism alone can confer the ephemeral enjoyment of them. The men who prize freedom only for such things as these are not men who ever long preserve it.

"That which at all times has so strongly attached the affection of certain men is the attraction of freedom herself, her native charms independent of her gifts—*the pleasure of speaking, acting, and breathing without restraint, under no master but God and the law* [the italics are ours]. He who seeks in freedom aught but herself is fit only to serve.

"There are nations which have indefatigably pursued her through every sort of peril and hardship. They loved her not for her material gifts; they regard herself as a gift so precious and so necessary that no other could console them for the loss of that which consoles them for the loss of everything else. Others grow weary of freedom in the midst of prosperities; they allow her to be snatched without resistance from their hands, lest they should sacrifice by an effort that well-being which she had bestowed upon them. For these to remain free, nothing was wanting but a taste for freedom. I attempt no analysis of that lofty sentiment to those who feel it not. It enters of its own accord into the large hearts God has prepared to receive it; it fills them, it enraptures them; but to the meaner minds which have never felt it, it is past finding out."[13] Under the yoke of Louis Napoleon's dictatorship he appealed to the perennial norms of freedom. It has been truly said that the nature of freedom is perceived more clearly when it is lacked than when it is possessed.

De Tocqueville always held fast to his belief in freedom, for freedom was a constituent element in his own nature.

No one before him described the danger of freedom's eclipse more incisively. In his early book on America he pointed with anxiety to the emergence of a plutocracy which would have the whiphand of the workers, exploit them, and make them soulless slaves of their machines. On the other hand the new plutocratic industrial despotism, oppressing the workers from above, might evoke an equally dangerous despotism from below. The workers would unite, conscious of their superiority in numbers, force higher wages from their exploiters until the day when they felt strong enough to impose on the plutocrats their own equalitarian tyranny, and thus ruthlessly put an end to the new aristocracy of money. Could there be any escape from this cycle?

Again and again, particularly in his later years, de Tocqueville attempted to draw a picture of the future of society in the West. "The grand problem of the future of our modern societies is constantly in my mind. It prevents me from seeing anything else or concentrating on any other object."[14] Did he really succeed in gaining a clear idea of it? He was firmly persuaded that "political societies are not the product of their laws, but are governed from the first by the feelings, modes of belief, ideas and habits of heart and mind of the people who live in them, and who in their turn are formed by nature and education."[15] The laws which comprise society are in a constant state of flux; can they ever be wholly destroyed and then re-erected? De Tocqueville asked himself this question, and he answered it as follows: "It seems to me impossible to carry this through. I say no more; for the more I study the world as it was, and the more I see in detail of the world as we have it to-day, the more I am impressed by the incredible differences one finds not only in the laws, but in the principles behind the laws, in the various forms which the right of property has, as one may say, assumed and maintained in the world; and I can well believe that what we call institutions are often only customary institutions, and that in constitutional questions the field of possibilities is much wider than the men who live in the bonds of any one particular social organization are able to imagine."[16] This passage occurs in the *Souvenirs,* and has a direct bearing on de Tocqueville's analysis of the different socialistic systems of his time.

It is not to be wondered at that his speculations found their limit here. The Archimedic point whence further journeyings were possible involved criticism of the principles of the bourgeois ordering of property, and this was begun a few years later by Karl Marx in *Das Kapital.*

De Tocqueville's view of things was focused on political life as a whole, wherein laws, institutions, sentiments, passions, ideas, and religious and moral customs and creeds are almost inextricably intertwined: a political philosophy such as Marx attempted to construct, and originating in the economic sphere in isolation, would have appeared to him an inadmissible abstraction. In actual fact Marxian socialism does lack that all-round penetration of political structures which de Tocqueville, although admittedly limited by the dying bourgeois world, took for granted.

EIGHT

Creed and Death

Freedom was de Tocqueville's political creed. This, however, did not make him a liberal. The liberal idea of the state was foreign to him—even contemptible. He detested the fat philistine who asked nothing of the state except to guarantee him a good night's rest. The freedom which concerned de Tocqueville was not license —freedom's anarchic caricature—but rather a regulated freedom, taking account of God's rule and God's everlasting laws.

A few passages from letters will illustrate this. "I wish that they [the priests] would say to them [their congregations] more often that, as well as being Christians, they belong to one or other of those great human associations which God has no doubt established to make more visible and more sensible the bonds which bind individuals together—*associations which men call 'nations' and their territories 'motherlands.' I could wish that they would instil into men's souls that each belongs to this collective being before he belongs to himself* [the italics are ours]; that in respect of this collective being there must be no indifference and still less must indifference be made into a kind of soft virtue which enervates some of the noblest instincts with which we are endowed; that all are responsible for what happens to the nation, and that all, according to their lights, are bound to work constantly for its prosperity and to watch that it be subject only to beneficent, honourable and legitimate authority."[1] It is plain here that de Tocqueville regards the nation as a divine creation, representing the strongest and most fundamental political bond for the individual. The nation to him is no contract as it was to Locke, the classic teacher of Western liberalism, but a bond of union by nature divine, and therefore something more than a code of laws.

State law is made by men. It may be imperfect and capricious, and do violence to human conscience. Man is then free to set up the law of his conscience against the law of the state, so that man's metaphysical norm again becomes the norm for the state.

De Tocqueville abhors those "who—be they advocates, judges, peasants, or soldiers—care for nothing beyond the small concerns which their own callings give rise to." Politics are a matter for passionate efforts. "You make my mouth water," he writes to Corcelle on October 11, 1846, "with your picture of the satisfaction there is to be found outside the political arena—no quarrels, no temptations, a contemplation of all things in an atmosphere of eternal serenity and impartiality. I tell you that I feel like beating you when I hear you talk like that! Good God, my dear friend, *that* is not politics! We have a goal that is great and good. How can we reach it without passionate effort . . . ?"[2] There is no mistaking a certain rigorism in de Tocqueville's political ethics. The Jansenist moralists influenced him profoundly through the writings of Pascal, but there is perhaps also a trace of Kant's influence which may have affected him through Royer-Collard. The categorical imperative of the great Prussian philosopher is by no means foreign to de Tocqueville's political philosophy.

This political philosophy was based on human nature in its totality, wherein politics, morality, and religion are fundamentally inseparable from one another. Just as with him the nation concept borders on the religious, so, on the other hand, religions and creeds are to him constituent categories in a healthy national life.

De Tocqueville's last years show an increasing consciousness of religion. Probably the steady decline of his health—the lung trouble, early apparent, having progressed to an acute and dangerous stage—made him more ready to receive the means of grace offered by the Roman Catholic Church, for serious illness often provides the motive in the history of religious conversions. Not that de Tocqueville had been irreligious up to this time. In early youth he had been touched by Cartesian skepticism, and in his outlook in maturity the chief stress was never laid on God and the things of religion. As a landowner he practiced the faith of his fathers, but as a convention rather than as a matter of personal devotion and belief. A letter of July 1835 to Kergorlay throws much light on the value he set upon the religious sphere in the human mind as a whole. "I have ever believed," he writes, "that there is danger even in the best passions when they become ardent and exclusive. I do not except the religious passion. . . . I place it first, in fact, because pressed to a certain point it obliterates, so to speak, everything but itself and makes very useless or very dangerous citizens in the name of morality and duty. I must confess to you that I have always *in petto* considered certain works of asceticism, regarded as anything else than text-books for the cloistered life, as dangerous in the extreme. [De Tocqueville refers here to Thomas a Kempis's *Imitation of Christ*.] It is not healthy to detach oneself from the world, its interests, its affairs, even its pleasures as long as these are virtuous ones, to the extent that these books teach; and those who live according to the doctrine of such books, while acquiring private virtues, can hardly fail to lose everything that makes for public virtue. *A real and vital preoccupation with religious truths which does not go to the length of complete absorption of the mind in the other world has always seemed to me the condition most conformable to human morality in all its forms* [the italics are ours]. This happy mean is achieved more often, I think, in this country than in that of any other people I know."[3] This letter was written on the occasion of a visit to Ireland.

In the third volume of *Democracy in America* de Tocqueville goes more closely into his sociological conception of religion, and rounds off the ideas formulated in the letter to Kergorlay. "In the ages of faith the final end of life is placed beyond life. The men of those ages therefore, naturally, and in a manner involuntarily, accustom themselves to fix their gaze for a long course of years on some immutable object towards which they are constantly tending; and they learn by insensible degrees to repress a multitude of

petty passing desires, in order to be the better able to satisfy that
great and lasting desire which possesses them. When these same
men engage in the affairs of this world, the same habits may be
traced in their conduct. They are apt to set up some general and
certain aim and end to their actions here below, towards which all
their efforts are directed: they do not turn from day to day to
chase some novel object of desire, but they have settled designs
which they are never weary of pursuing.

"This explains why religious nations have so often achieved
such lasting results: for whilst they were thinking only of the
other world, they had found out the great secret of success in
this. . . .

"Governments must apply themselves to restore to men that
love of the future with which religion and the state of society no
longer inspire them; and, without saying so, they must practically
teach the community day by day that wealth, fame, and power
are the rewards of labour—that great success stands at the utmost
range of long desires, and that nothing lasting is obtained but
what is obtained by toil. . . . Thus the means which allow men,
up to a certain point, to go without religion, are perhaps after all
the only means we still possess for bringing mankind back by a
long and roundabout path to a state of faith."[4] De Tocqueville
clearly recognized the antireligious tendency in the modern state.
This has much increased since his day, and may probably even be
regarded as permanent, unless some great crisis in the West, such
as might be brought about any day now by war, were to bring in
its train a revival of religion.

De Tocqueville ended his life as a believing Catholic. His work
was finished, and he was able to listen to the inner voice of conscience bidding him make his peace with the God of his fathers.
Such is my own interpretation of de Tocqueville's conversion, the
story of which is convincingly told in the closing chapter of the
book by Redier which I have so frequently quoted here. Of the
new, unpublished documents which Redier has so devotedly assembled in this chapter I will only quote one letter to Mme.
Swetchine, bearing the date of February 26, 1857, and most

essential to an understanding of de Tocqueville's religious development. "I believe that my sentiments and my desires are in excess
of my capacities. I believe that God has given me a natural taste
for great actions and great virtues, and that despair at never being
able to lay hold on the grand vision that floats before my eyes, the
sadness of living in a world and an epoch that answers so little to
that ideal creation in which my spirit loves to dwell—I believe,
I say, that these impressions which age does nothing to weaken,
are among the chief causes of this interior *malaise* of which I
have never been able to get the better. But to how many less
reputable causes must I not attribute it also!"[5] Finally de Tocqueville confesses to his friend his ambitions as a writer, possessed by
the passion for success and renown—a passion which, as he admits, reawoke in him with the publication of his book on the
Revolution. "What an absurd cause for agitation! But here is
another, perhaps worthy of pity—the incessant and always vain
effort of a spirit which aspires to certitude and cannot lay hold on
it, which needs it more than another perhaps, yet less than another can enjoy it in peace. The problem of human existence
preoccupies me ceaselessly, and ceaselessly appalls me. I can
neither plumb this mystery nor cease to peer into it. It excites me
and oppresses me by turns. . . . I find human life in this world
inexplicable, and in the other terrifying. I firmly believe in a
future life because God, who is perfectly just, has given us this
concept, and I believe that in this other life good and evil will be
recompensed, since God permits us to distinguish between them
and has given us liberty to choose. But, these distinct ideas apart,
everything beyond the frontiers of this world seems to me
shrouded in a darkness which affrights me. . . ."[6] I can break
off here, since I have dealt already with further points raised in
this letter in my interpretation of de Tocqueville's spiritual and
moral life.

During the last few weeks of mortal illness at Cannes de
Tocqueville listened, deeply moved, to the words of the gospel
which his nurses read to him. He confessed to his brother his grief
that religion had not occupied a larger place in his life. "If God

gives me back my health I am resolved to consecrate myself to it with more ardour."[7]

Alexis de Tocqueville confessed his sins and received the grace-giving sacraments of the Catholic Church, the church of his fathers. On April 16, 1859, he passed into eternity.

NINE

Legacy

A prophet is without honor in his own country, and the history of de Tocqueville's influence in France has, in fact, been subject to continuous misunderstanding. He was classified as a *political* liberal until Redier's discovery of him as a great "Liberal of a new kind." His contemporaries paid him homage as "a virtuous and honourable Liberal"—Mignet in a fine memorial address, Sainte-Beuve in his *Causeries du Lundi,* Guizot in a speech before the Académie Française—so that even after death de Tocqueville remained misunderstood. Since the great French Revolution, party labels have often supplied names that hide the truth. Even that noteworthy study, "Alexis de Tocqueville et la science politique au XIXe siècle," by Paul Janet,[1] learned historian of Western political theory, by no means amounts to an all-round appreciation of de Tocqueville's significance. Nonetheless, de Tocqueville's political opinions are clearly distinguished in this study from the doctrines of French liberalism. "What the Liberal school called the despotism of democracy was demagogic violence, the brutal and savage government of the masses. But de Tocqueville had in mind another kind of despotism, not that of militant democracy, driven in the heat of conflict to acts of violence which, though abominable, manifest a certain savage grandeur. No, he envisaged democracy at rest, successively leveling down and abasing all individuals, putting its fingers into all kinds of interests, imposing uniform and petty rules on every one, treating men as abstractions, subjecting society to a mechanical movement, and

ending by reposing itself in the absolute power of one man."
Janet also sees clearly that de Tocqueville is utterly opposed to
the liberal school of his day in his absolute insistence on decentralization within the community. In Janet's summing-up,
however, de Tocqueville appears merely as a publicist or as a
philosophizing politician: Janet feels constrained to dismiss the
possibility of his being a genuine political philosopher. Since then
the perspective of time has enabled us to recognize the uniqueness
of de Tocqueville's intellectual rank.

In 1897 Eugène d'Eichthal wrote his *Tocqueville and Liberal
Democracy,* and Émile Faguet added to his *Politiques et Moralistes du dix-neuvième siècle* a study of the *patricien libéral.*
Neither work gave an adequate picture of the great political
sociologist whose only party was the party of Truth. In 1910
Marcel published a thesis for a doctorate on de Tocqueville and
for this purpose he had access to the family archives, but although
this book expressly undertakes to place de Tocqueville in the
framework of his times, it betrays, in a certain easy familiarity of
manner, a complete failure to grasp his greatness, and it shows a
corresponding readiness to correct his ideas.

Stronger, however, than the literary influence I have sum-
marily mentioned was what one might call de Tocqueville's
subterranean influence. This is particularly recognizable in Proudhon, through whom it touches Marx (though very indirectly),
and, most emphatically, in Georges Sorel. Le Play was influenced
by de Tocqueville in a negative sense. He thought his book on
America a dangerous work that had done a great deal of harm.

Sorel, in his *Illusions du progrès,* shows how Proudhon's *Contradictions économiques* was inspired by the egalitarian principle
as formulated by de Tocqueville, and earlier writings of Proudhon's, such as *La Célébration du Dimanche* (1839) and his first
memoir on *Property* (1840), show, as Sorel proves, the influence
of the author of *Democracy in America.* This memoir was well
known to Marx and Engels, as is apparent in *The Holy Family,*
of which they were joint authors. In Marx's *Poverty of Philosophy,* an attack on Proudhon's *Contradictions,* he employs his

special brand of bitter and malicious irony against the view which Proudhon shares with de Tocqueville of the "providential character" of the egalitarian principle, and describes Proudhon as a belated disciple of Bossuet. The taunt is equally applicable to de Tocqueville.

This is not the place to inquire how far Marx understood or misunderstood Proudhon—or, perhaps, it would be truer to say, *chose* to understand or misunderstand him.

"Of course, the tendency towards equality," schoolmaster Karl Marx teaches his undutiful pupil Proudhon, whom he had tried in vain to familiarize with the mysteries of Hegelian dialectics during long and passionate discussions in Paris, "belongs to our century. To say now that all former centuries, with entirely different needs, means of production, etc., worked providentially for the realization of equality, is, firstly, to substitute the means and the men of our century for the men and the means of earlier centuries and to misunderstand the historical movement by which the successive generations transformed the results acquired by the generations that preceded them."[2] Here Marx's view is, of course, quite right, and de Tocqueville would scarcely have contradicted him. It remains an open question whether Proudhon properly understood de Tocqueville. Furthermore, at that time the author of *Democracy in America* had a wider and more thorough knowledge of history than Marx, and was aware, as Marx was not, that the egalitarian tendency in Western history made its appearance in late medieval times, not first in the nineteenth century. The providential character of the principle of equality lies, as we have seen, at the root of de Tocqueville's religious outlook, which saw mankind as the free and equal creatures of God. It is in this sense alone that democracy is providential. Marx himself, as we know, describes the socialistic ordering of society as one of freedom and equality. He saw less clearly than did de Tocqueville that in principle and aim his social philosophy was founded in Western Christianity.

Sorel, in this connection, identified himself with Marx with this one difference, that he refers Marx's criticism to de Tocqueville.

He reproaches the author of *Democracy in America* because his description of the social constitution of America answers by no means exactly to the truth of things in 1908, the year of the publication of the *Illusions*. "No traveller visiting the United States to-day will admire the conditions of equality which the French writer noticed there in 1832; America was then an agrarian country; to-day it is an industrial country; speculation has brought into existence there incredible inequalities."[3] Whoever has followed the argument of this book so far will admit that de Tocqueville's analysis of American class relationships, far from overlooking these facts, expressly foretold them. In de Tocqueville's view it is just these "incredible inequalities" of which Sorel speaks that challenge the workers to a most radical application of the egalitarian principle.

If Sorel is critical of de Tocqueville's position in this instance he nonetheless quite definitely owes much to him on other points. Not only Sorel's estimate of the nature of the French Revolution, but still more his ethical conception of history, shows a deep, as it were atmospheric, intimacy with de Tocqueville's doctrines.

These few remarks should be enough, I think, to give an approximate idea of the extent of his influence in the intellectual history of France. Today in his own country even the *Œuvres complètes* are out of print, and not one Frenchman has come forward to dedicate a new and more worthy edition of his works to one of the greatest sons of France.*

In the England of de Tocqueville's own times John Stuart Mill and Nassau Senior have the great merit of having understood de Tocqueville's significance. As we have seen Mill celebrated him as the great modern philosopher of democracy. Through Mill's writings de Tocqueville exercised considerable influence on English and American political science. Senior dedicated his fine work, *Correspondence and Conversations* to him. But up to the

---

* Since this work was written Messrs. Gallimard, Paris, have decided to publish a new edition of de Tocqueville's principal works and letters, under my direction. Of this edition, eight volumes have now (1959) been published.

present, even in the land of political biography *par excellence,* there is not a single book on the thinker who interpreted the English political and social constitution more deeply than anyone since Burke. The reason for this curious phenomenon may lie perhaps in the Englishman's dislike of introspection. De Tocqueville brought to the light of consciousness too many of the characteristics of English political life—a consciousness which is foreign to the *occasional* nature of the English habit of thought. Harold J. Laski, in a brilliant essay which must on no account pass unmentioned, says that de Tocqueville and Lord Acton should be regarded as "the essential Liberals of the nineteenth century," whereby unfortunately the distinguished English professor of political science makes the mistake of classifying de Tocqueville under a party label even while his own analysis explodes the fallacy. For he writes of de Tocqueville: "His sense that an individualistic economy and a political democracy are incompatible has been justified by all subsequent history. . . . He saw that the privileges of property are an inherent contradiction of popular sovereignty, and that they involve either surrender by their possessors or challenge by those excluded from them."[4] In this passage Laski hits the nail very neatly on the head, but he fails to see that a thinker in whose political philosophy this recognition plays an essential part must already have overstepped in principle the boundaries of liberalism. There is nothing quietistic about such a confession of faith: it implies a step forward into a *new* world.

In America Francis Lieber has paid understanding tribute to the great analyst of American political life, and in the third volume of his *Political Theories* Dunning has devoted some able pages to de Tocqueville, though these do not in any sense penetrate the fundamentals of his political philosophy.[5]

In the literature of political science in Germany Robert von Mohl and J. C. Bluntschli have done the service of making due mention of de Tocqueville's significance. In Mohl's *History and Literature of the Political Sciences,* whose first volume appeared in 1855, de Tocqueville is classed among "the first of political scientists,"[6] and Bluntschli, in his *Geschichte des allgemeinen*

Staatsrechts und der Politik (1864), states that de Tocqueville's books "have exercised on German political science an influence which may be traced, but which is less than the actual value of the works would lead one to expect."[7] Late in the seventies Karl Hillebrand, in a little-known but nonetheless important work entitled *The History of France from Louis Philippe's Accession to the Fall of Napoleon III* (unfortunately it breaks off unfinished after the fall of Louis Philippe), remarks on the great importance of de Tocqueville. Hillebrand is to be counted among the few Europeans of the nineteenth century to whom the wealth of the German, English, and French cultures were alike a natural possession, among the few also who gave public support to the warning voice of Friedrich Nietzsche, first prophet of the nihilism invading Europe. Of de Tocqueville he wrote the remarkable sentences which follow, though they seem to have been unable to ruffle the phlegmatic optimism in matters of political theory which characterized the dying seventies of the last century. "The times were not ready to listen to him," wrote Hillebrand of the great Frenchman, "or only half understood him, divided as they were between the wish to preserve the old, even though it was dead, and to institute the new, even though it was not yet born; doctrinaires and friends of revolution alike saw an enemy to that fair unity and ordering of France which, as they thought had been created by the great Revolution, in the man who, little troubled about questions of monarchy, republic, veto, ministerial responsibility, etc., posed the question as to how existing democracy might best be educated and organized for self-rule so that it should not, as so often in history, degenerate into despotism. . . . He was not even to see his view of things find acceptance with the educated part of the nation. . . . Filled as he was with a high and fine culture, he saw with clear eyes the inevitable mediocrity of the democracy destined for rule. He guessed, as Royer-Collard told him, that in the future State which he foresaw there would not be so many as ten readers to understand his book; but he wanted to show both the doctrinaires and the waverers that what was inevitable might, at least, be peaceably brought about, and

how. . . . For the moment the most important, or at any rate
the most enduring, achievement of the thirties and forties amused
the majority as a witty paradox which interrupted the monoto-
nous commonplace of politics, but did not prevent the most extreme conceptions of the State from gaining increasing hold on
the dissatisfied element of the community. . . ."[8] With a few
exceptions European readers were still unripe for a fruitful appreciation of the wealth of the great French political scientist's
thought. In our own day, after renewed experience of a dangerous breaking of the dams under pressure of the rising tide of the
plebiscitary masses, the historical experience of the last century
has drawn appreciably nearer.

The Italian historian G. de Ruggiero, in his instructive *History
of European Liberalism,* recognizes de Tocqueville as the most
important writer of the period of the July Monarchy, "perhaps
the greatest produced by France in the nineteenth century."
Ruggiero has a sure instinct for the uniqueness of intellectual
rank to be assigned to de Tocqueville.[9]

In remarking thus briefly on the influence of de Tocqueville's
works in England, America, Germany, and Italy it has not been
at all my intention to anticipate some future historian in the task
of estimating the great French philosopher's influence. My main
object throughout has been to present the content of Alexis de
Tocqueville's political philosophy with a running commentary,
and I hope that my work will shortly be followed by other and
more broadly based treatments of the subject.

The time is ripe for an understanding of de Tocqueville. Any
such more comprehensive research must natuarlly go more deeply
than I have done into the intellectual influences affecting his
thought, more especially his relationship to Edmund Burke and
Royer-Collard. On this subject a few words may, however, be in
place here. It is not difficult to discover from a careful reading
of *The Ancien Régime and the Revolution* that it is in one aspect
a running commentary upon Burke's *Reflections on the French
Revolution.* De Tocqueville, I think, quotes from Burke more
often and more exhaustively in this book than from any other

writer in all the rest of his works. But the differences between the two thinkers are greater than those ideas which they have in common. Both are profoundly religious, and are agreed that states lacking the secure foundation of a religious belief are doomed to destruction. They also agree in emphasizing the traditional factor in the historical development of the state. But whereas Burke regards full-blown traditions as a persistent norm, and assigns a merely circumferential role to the formative ratio in matters political, the Frenchman brings out the motive force of this ratio which may indeed be destructive, but which must not on that account be denied the force of fact. "Government by prescription" was Burke's motto, but de Tocqueville shows, though without becoming an apostle of the doctrine of progress, how the dynamic force of the process of democratization in the West eventually breaks through traditional norms and orders, thereby setting modern states and societies quite new tasks, and casting into the melting pot the very constitutive elements of these societies. Burke hated and combated the French Revolution, and was indeed its most formidable opponent. De Tocqueville certainly did not love the Revolution, yet he recognized in it the new principles for the nineteenth and twentieth centuries.

Royer-Collard, who belonged to de Tocqueville's father's generation, was probably the most important political thinker of the period of the restoration of the monarchy.[10] He had sat in the Revolutionary National Assembly, and the Jacobin dictatorship nearly sent him to the guillotine. He was a member of the Council of State under Louis XVIII, and for a short period president of the Chamber. He was a great orator, an important writer, the true political philosopher of the 1814 constitution. He set himself the task of endeavoring to reconcile the monarchical and revolutionary forces of the French nation. His very interesting correspondence with de Tocqueville shows that he willingly conceded to his younger friend the ability to formulate the principles of the new democratic age.

From Royer-Collard's school comes the well-known dictum:

la démocratie coule à pleins bords. De Tocqueville systematized this dictum.

Royer-Collard recognized before de Tocqueville the dangers of a majority tyranny in the egalitarian and centralistic structure of postrevolutionary France. He reflected on the political guarantees of human freedom, and made freedom of the press, tolerance of religious beliefs, the independence of the judicature and, finally, parliamentary privilege, indispensable political demands for the countering of absolutism. He distinguished penetratingly between parliamentary and representative government; the latter he held to be possible only under universal suffrage and he rejected this. Here de Tocqueville disagreed with him. The younger man insisted on the voluntary character of a parliamentary regime. The *Charte* of 1814, after the July revolution, belonged to the irrevocable past, but the dangers of universal suffrage, so acutely analyzed by Royer-Collard, remained always before de Tocqueville's eyes.

Even the "atmospheric" definition of freedom, already discussed in this book, finds unmistakable expression in Royer-Collard's writings.

No doubt enough has been said to show the important influence which Royer-Collard exercised upon de Tocqueville, yet it amounted only to stimulus, perhaps necessary as such in laying the foundations of his thought. It does not detract from the weight and originality of his political philosophy.

La démocratie coule à pleins bords. The rising of the masses is written in the destiny of our societies. De Tocqueville's political philosophy was a prophecy, a burden, and a warning. He shared the burden with many a great man of his century, for it was felt alike by Goethe, Jacob Burckhardt, Nietzsche, Georges Sorel, and Max Weber.[10a] Possibly Max Weber's work offers the most congenial recapitulation of de Tocqueville's formulation of the problem, differing only in a more universal purview of the question, since Weber takes account of the Eastern cultures also, and in the disillusioned gaze of an age which had cast off religion.[11] In 1906 Max Weber wrote the following prophetic words. "Everywhere the framework of a new bondage is ready, waiting only for the slowing down of technical 'progress,' and for the victory of 'interest' over 'profit,' in combination with exhaustion of as yet 'free' territory and 'free' markets, to make the masses tractable to its compulsion. At the same time the increasing complexity of the economic system, its partial nationalization or 'municipal- ization,' and the territorial magnitude of national organisms, is creating ever more clerical work, an increasing specialization of labour and professional training in administration—and this means the creation of a bureaucratic caste. . . . Whatever spheres of 'inalienable' personality and freedom are still unwon by the common people in the course of the next few generations, and while the economic and intellectual 'revolution,' the much- maligned 'anarchy' of production, and the equally maligned 'sub- jectivism' (by which, and *by which alone,* the individual has been made self-dependent) still remain unbroken, may *perhaps*—once the world has become economically 'full' and intellectually 'sated'—remain unachieved by them, for as far as our weak eyes can pierce the impenetrable mists of the future of man- kind. . . ."[12] Today, more than thirty years later, the threat to human freedom in the mass societies of the Western nations is more acute than ever. Not even Max Weber was ready radically to question the property basis of the bourgeois world. He was nearer to de Tocqueville than to Karl Marx.

It would be a complete misunderstanding of the meaning of my interpretation of de Tocqueville's political philosophy if it were to be supposed that we are to look for the necessary correc- tive of his doctrines in the alternative of a dogmatic adoption of the Marxian position. Marx did indeed inaugurate economic criticism of the bourgeois social order, but he showed little under- standing of the problems of institutional and political organization in the modern mass state. He taught the gradual dying-off of the state, whereas historical experience has since demonstrated the contrary—a mighty increase in power of the political executive. Even a socialistic order, provided its members are men and not angels, will always contain some that govern and some that are governed. Must the politically *governing,* then—one is bound to ask the question—be always ready as a matter of course to surrender their power as soon as the *governed* wish it? Or will not those who lead always assert that they use their political power simply in the interests of the led, however little the facts support their contention? The moral aspect is never simple. Marx was never concerned with this difficulty of a political elite. His utopian faith in the better (more rational) judgment of Communist leaders showed his lack of comprehension of the many-sidedness of political man. Burke assigned the task of running the state to a "natural aristocracy" which, it cannot be denied, bore a remarkable resemblance in character to the Whigs of his day.

Perhaps the great weakness of de Tocqueville's political philosophy is that it evaded this problem. Not that he failed to perceive it. In a letter of December 5, 1835, to John Stuart Mill he touched on the difficulties in principle of a political elite. "I know not one friend of democracy who has yet dared to bring out in so precise and clear a manner the capital distinction between *delegation* and *representation,* or who has better fixed the political sense of the two words. Rest assured, my dear Mill, that you have touched there a question of the first magnitude—at least such is my firm conviction. It is a lesser question for the partisans of democracy to find means of governing the people than to *get the people to choose the men most capable of governing* [the italics are ours], and to give them in addition power enough to direct the latter in matters as a whole, but not in the details of their work nor the means of execution. *That is the problem. I am fully convinced that upon its solution depends the fate of the modern nations* [the italics are ours]."[13] De Tocqueville formulated the problem, but he did not solve it. His presuppositions made it impossible for him to do so. The aristocracy as a political elite had been annihilated. A bourgeoisie, unheroic and caring only for security and easy living, into whose rights and claims fresh masses of the populace were continually pressing their way (a process which has by no means reached a standstill in our day)—such a bourgeoisie was devoid of all political virtue. A political elite recruited from the bourgeoisie seemed to de Tocqueville merely a *contradictio in adiecto;* he saw no possible basis for a political elite fit to be trusted with the leadership of the state save in a mixture of bourgeois elements with those of the nobility and the "people," such as English society had produced and might be able to preserve into the future. This, however, was to give only an interpretation of the realities of the English social system. The problem first becomes a burning one when England's special historical background is *not* among the conditions.

Georges Sorel was the earliest to draw the logical conclusion from de Tocqueville's premises, and to teach belief in a proletarian elite which should not take the bourgeoisie for its model, but should build on its own primitive and unused powers. The seductions of the bourgeoisie are, however, great. The spirit is willing but the flesh is weak. Our historical experience of the erection of new kinds of political societies in the nations of the West is still too much in flux for us to be justified in pronouncing anything definite in respect of contemporary elites. It may someday be possible to reconcile the postulate of freedom with the modern egalitarian mass society.

Such a society, in some far and uncertain future, ought to erect a memorial to Alexis de Tocqueville.

Tocqueville After a Century*

Tocqueville died on the 16th of April, 1859. After the lapse of one hundred years, it is right, and even necessary, that we ask ourselves the question: what is his permanent contribution to a political sociology?

It is well known that the two first volumes of the *Democracy in America,* which appeared in 1835, already assured him of a first ranking among the political writers of his time. Sainte-Beuve commented in the *Revue des Deux Mondes* of April 7, 1835: "A complete survery of M. de Tocqueville's book would provide matter for the examination of all capital questions of modern politics. . . . However, in praising such a recently published book, one is only voicing the already established judgment [of it] by all competent authorities in the field. The approval of Chateaubriand, of Royer-Collard, of Lamartine, was expressed strongly enough for us to record it without fear of letting ourselves be deceived by polite superficialities. We would have to go very far back to find [among us] a book of science and political observation which aroused the attention and satisfied thinkers to such a degree."[1]

Today it seems that it was only with the publication of the last two volumes of the *Democracy in America* that Tocqueville showed his real greatness. (They appeared in 1840.) However,

---

* A public lecture delivered before the annual meeting of the American society for French Historical Studies at Cleveland, Ohio, and in slightly modified form at Princeton University (April, 1959).

Sainte-Beuve was, according to all evidence, less enthusiastic with respect to them and judged them as follows:

"For almost ten years since he left America, that country has served no more than as a pretext for the author, no more than a man of straw; he is speaking to modern societies, to France as much as to America. His thesis is the effects and dangers of equality in all conditions and civic relations within a democratic society and it is here that one feels its inferiority as compared with Montesquieu. The author lacks examples to illustrate or animate his pages."[2]

Tocqueville himself in a certain measure shared the opinion of the great critic, for we read in a letter to John Stuart Mill: "The success of this second part of the *Democracy* was a less popular one in France than that of the first. . . . I am therefore very pre-occupied with searching into myself, as to what error I have fallen subject, for it is probable that there is a considerable one. I believe that the fault I seek is to be found in the very basis of the book which expresses something obscure and problematic which does not move the mass. When I spoke only of democratic society in the United States it was immediately understood. If I had spoken of our democratic society in France, [such] as it shows itself in our day, this would also be well understood. But on leaving the ideas which American and French Society presented me, *I wished to set out the general tendencies of democratic societies of which no complete example yet exists.* . . ."[3]

The last phrase of Tocqueville's is decisive (I have permitted myself to italicize it). For a reader of the rank and of the perspicacity of Sainte-Beuve, the sociological method, which Max Weber was to use with such success, remained incomprehensible. Tocqueville had already set up what Weber called "the ideal type." That is to say, a sociological notion nourished by social reality and at the same time typified. This method gives the last volumes of the *Democracy* their contemporary character. John Stuart Mill understood this so well that in a memorable article published in the *Edinburgh Review* the English philosopher wrote of the completed work of Tocqueville as "the first philosophical book ever written on Democracy as it manifests itself in modern society; a book, the essential doctrines of which it is not likely that any future generations will subvert, to whatever degree they may modify them; while its spirit, and the general mode in which it treats its subject, constitute the beginning of a new era in the scientific study of politics."[4]

That which in 1840 appeared far distant or, as Sainte-Beuve said, "without example," has in 1959 become our present or immediate future.

It is necessary to reread the fourth part of the last volume of the *Democracy in America* to understand well the acuteness and depth of Tocqueville's analysis.

"As long as the democratic revolution was glowing with heat, the men who were bent upon the destruction of aristocratic powers hostile to that revolution displayed a strong spirit of independence; but as the victory of the principle of equality became more complete, they gradually surrendered themselves to the propensities natural to that condition of equality, and they strengthened and centralized their governments. They had sought to be free in order to make themselves equal; but in proportion as equality was more established by the aid of freedom, freedom itself was thereby rendered more difficult of attainment."[5]

Tocqueville's sociological analysis does not only reveal our past, it also penetrates the clouds of the future and describes our present. The new society is everywhere around us:

"A multitude of similar and equal individuals are working to procure themselves petty and vulgar satisfactions. Above these men there rears a monstrous tutelary power who provides for their security, foresees and supplies their necessities, directs their industry, regulates the descent of property, and subdivides their inheritances: what remains, but to spare them all the care of thinking and all the trouble of living."[6]

The anticipation of what then was but a tendency gave Tocqueville that feeling of solitude which he sometimes expressed in his correspondence with his most intimate friends. "We are the last of the last." Or, as Lord Acton, his spiritual relative in England, often said a little later: "I have no contemporaries."

Indeed, Tocqueville remained alone all his life. Apart from his wife, an English lady who understood him through love and intuition, and Madame Swetchine, with whom there existed a deep understanding on the religious plane during his last years, nobody, not even Beaumont, Reeve, Mill, Jean-Jacques Ampère, or Kergorlay, among others, entered into the subtle structure of Tocqueville's thought.

It is an irresistible temptation to evoke here that great figure, the Swiss historian Jacob Burckhardt, who, influenced by Tocqueville in his conception of history, equally predicted the totalitarian state within the near future.

"The military state is bound to become a big manufacturer. These agglomerations of men in the great factories are bound not to remain in poverty and greed. A degree of definite and superintended poverty where everyone would have his promotion guaranteed and would wear the uniform and where the day would begin and end with the drum-roll; logically this is what should come."[7] These prophetic lines may be read in a letter from Burckhardt dated 1872. A few years later the great Swiss historian wrote to the same friend: "The education of the young with a view to making them used to large crowds is begun very early. The result will be that people will start crying when there are not about a hundred of them together."[8] It is only today in the epoch of the cinema and of television that we are taking note of the bearing of Tocqueville's thought.

Some ten years ago I tried to show in a book on the *Sociology of Film* how our emotions—indeed, our very instincts—are stultified and stereotyped by commercial movies; how they make our children greedy or how they burden their young souls with unnecessary and artificial shocks and horrors. Here, for your country, Fredric Wertham and David Riesman, the latter much influenced by Tocqueville, directed our attention to the same dangers: perhaps, if I am not mistaken, our labors were not in vain. For in my country as in yours a new cultural nonconformism seems to have come to life: the plant is still young and weak, but it may gather in strength with years to come provided we persevere. Perhaps, after all, William Whyte's *Organization Man* is not the last word on the present historic moment: perhaps, guided by such examples as Tocqueville, we may regain our ability to live and suffer and above all to create in loneliness.

> Und wenn der Mensch in seiner Qual verstummt
> Gab ihm ein Gott die Kraft zu sagen, was er leidet

If we compare the political sociology of Tocqueville with that of Karl Marx, who was thirteen years his junior, it is evident that Tocqueville's thought is far from being a humanitarian utopianism. Certainly there are common points between the two thinkers. "All history until the present," Marx wrote in the *Communist Manifesto,* "is that of class struggles." In Tocqueville's *Ancien Régime* we read (on p. 179 of our edition[9]): "I speak of classes, they alone would preoccupy history." Similarly, both thinkers have taught us that the French revolution of 1789 is only a *phase* in the history of social revolutions of the nineteenth century; other revolutions have followed and will follow. Or, as we read in Marx's *Eighteenth Brumaire:* "Bourgeois revolutions like those of the eighteenth century speed from success to success; they vie with one another in the lustre of their stage effects; men and things seem to be set in sparkling brilliants; every day is filled with ecstasy: but they are shortlived; their climax is soon reached; on the morning after, society has to pass through a long fit of storm and stress. Proletarian revolutions, on the other hand, like those of the nineteenth century, are ever self-critical; they again and again stop short in their progress; retrace their steps in order to make a fresh start; are pitilessly scornful of the half-measures, the weaknesses, the futility of their preliminary attempts. It seems as if they have overthrown their adversaries only in order that these might draw renewed strength from contact with the earth, and return to the battle like giants refreshed. Again and again, they shrink back appalled before the vague immensity of their own aims. But, at long last, a situation is reached whence retreat is impossible, and where the circumstances clamour in chorus:

Hic Rhodus, Hic salta!
Here is the Rose; dance here!"[10]

But the relation between Tocqueville and Marx stops there. Tocqueville has none of the absolutism of Marx. "For my part," Tocqueville wrote in his *Souvenirs,* "I detest these absolute systems, which represent all the events of history as depending upon great causes linked by the chain of fatality, and which, as it were, suppress men from the history of the human race. Antecedent facts, the nature of institutions, the cast of minds and the state of morals are the materials of which are composed those impromptus which astonish and alarm us."[11] In addition, Marx's conception of a classless society is incompatible with Tocqueville's idea that Western societies are moving toward an increasingly egalitarian structure; for within the society of the future Tocqueville anticipated a new class structure that is shaping itself.

I should like to say at this point that, having just reread volume two of the *Democracy in America,* I find that Tocqueville is perhaps not quite as clear-cut on this important point as my paper suggests. Though he indicates in Chapter XX, part I (*"Comment l'Aristocratie pourrait sortir de l'Industrie"*), the aristocratic tendencies of highly industrialized societies, it would seem that Chapter XXVI of Part III contradicts this statement: "Under a caste regime, one generation succeeds another without men changing place; they neither wait for anything more, nor expect anything better. Their imagination sleeps in the midst of a silent and universal immobility, and the idea of change does not even suggest itself to the human spirit.

"But when classes are abolished and conditions have become almost equal, all men agitate ceaselessly; but each one is alone, independent, and vulnerable. This last state differs prodigiously from the first, but is analogous to it in one point: great revolutions of the human spirit are very rare." There is another footnote in Chapter XXVI of the same part of the *Democracy* which ex-

presses the same view: "When the state of society among a people
is democratic—that is, when castes or classes no longer exist in
the community, and its members are nearly equal in education
and in property—the human mind follows the opposite direction.
Men are much alike, and they are annoyed, as it were, by any
deviation from that likeness; far from seeking to preserve their
own distinguishing singularities, they endeavor to shake them off
in order to identify themselves with the general mass of the people,
which is the sole representative of right and might to their eyes.
The spirit of individuality is almost obliterated."

Tocqueville's formula *quand les classes ont été abolies* has,
however, a different meaning than Marx's classless society.
Whereas the classless society—according to Marx—is the realm of
the free and equal, Tocqueville's "classless" society is one which
by establishing equality or near-equality has destroyed freedom.
It is the task of politics to devise mechanisms to safeguard man's
liberties.

Though one is bound to say that the great Frenchman understood as Marx did that the social revolutions of the nineteenth
century had the struggle for property as their theme, the Tocque-
villean sociology is more pliable in respect to this tendency.
Tocqueville asks himself in a page of his *Souvenirs:*

"Will Socialism remain buried in the disdain with which the
Socialists of 1848 are so justly covered? I put the question without
making a reply. I do not doubt that the laws concerning the
constitution of our modern society will in the long run undergo
modification; they have already done so in many of their principal
parts. But will they ever be destroyed and replaced by others?
It seems to me to be impracticable. I say no more, because the
more I study the former condition of the world and see the world
of our own day in greater detail, the more I consider the prodigious variety to be met with not only in laws, but in the principles
of law, and the different forms even now taken and retained,
whatever one may say, by the rights of property on this earth,
the more I am tempted to believe that what we call necessary institutions are often no more than institutions to which we

have grown accustomed, and that in matters of social constitution the field of possibilities is much more extensive than men living in their various societies are ready to imagine."[12]

It may be seen with what prudence Tocqueville's thought bends itself under the pressure of social complexity.

While Marxism taught the slow death of the state—one of the most dangerous and fallacious utopias which could have been invented—the *Democracy in America* supplied us with a precise description of the very substance of the modern state as it surrounds us everywhere. "In proportion as the functions of the central power are augmented, the number of public offices representing that power must increase also. They form a nation, within each nation; and as they share the stability of the government, they more and more fill up the place of an aristocracy."[13] It was evident to Tocqueville that this was a European phenomenon: "I assert that there is no country in Europe in which the public administration has not become, not only more centralized, but more inquisitive and more minute: everywhere it interferes in private concerns more than it did; it regulates more undertakings, and undertakings of a lesser kind; and it gains a firmer footing every day, about, above, and around all private persons, to assist, to advise, and to coerce them."[14] In fact the state does not appear to be slowly dying.

It is certain that Tocqueville was not the first modern political writer who had analyzed the phenomenon of administrative centralization. Chéruel examined it almost at the same time as he; Dareste de La Chavanne and Béchard preceded him; but Tocqueville was the first to have a presentiment of the dangers of administrative centralization for the condition of man; moreover his paramount aim was to suggest institutional devices to safeguard the soul of man rather than to protect his economic security. There it seems that he was under the influence of his father, Hervé de Tocqueville, who married the granddaughter of Lamoignon de Malesherbes. Tocqueville inherited the legacy of the great liberal magistrates and administrators of the eighteenth century which was directed against the pernicious administrative absolutism of the Old Order.

It has always seemed capital to me that Tocqueville could give a description and a definition of the modern state but could not find a name for this monster: "It is a new thing, it is therefore necessary to attempt to define it as I cannot name it."[15] Would he perhaps have found the name *managerial state* acceptable? Without a doubt Tocqueville's sociology analyzes the state and modern society in a more adequate manner than does Burnham or more recently Hans Freyer (who has, however, reminded us of the greatness of Tocqueville).[16]

It is not surprising that the political thought of the great sociologist could not form a school. Almost always in the history of political thought only the secondary or inessential ideas become widespread. This was the case with Montesquieu, whose theory of the separation of powers had an enormous influence in Europe and America, though this theory hides rather than reveals the real substance of Montesquieu's sociology. As far as Tocqueville is concerned we are up against the same phenomenon. Barthélemy assures us in his *Treatise on Constitutional Law* (Paris, 1933, p. 46): "The political education of the generation which produced the constitution of 1875 was based a little on Proudhon, a great deal on the *Democracy in America* and lastly and above all on the works . . . of de Broglie and Prévost-Paradol."[17] As in the case of Montesquieu only the constitutional mechanisms of the first two volumes of this great work touched this generation. The substance of Tocqueville's political sociology remained almost uncomprehended. It is we who have to perform this task.

Perhaps we should ask ourselves whether the historians of the nineteenth century showed a more adequate appreciation of Tocqueville. Without a doubt his *Ancien Régime and the Revolution,* the first edition of which appeared in 1856, had a great influence on French and non-French historiography. I have already mentioned Burckhardt; I might add Ranke and Sybel, and in England Acton, not to mention other German historians. With Dilthey, however, we reach a different plane. His was the nearest to a contemporary valuation of Tocqueville. It is sufficient to mention Taine, Fustel de Coulanges or Albert Sorel; but Tocqueville is not an historian in the *narrow* sense of the term; *Ancien Régime* is more a sociological work than a specialized study of the French Revolution. Once more it is Tocqueville himself who best explains to us the intention of his work: "You know, for a long time," he writes to Gustave Beaumont from Sorrento on the 10th of January, 1851, "I have been pre-occupied with the idea of undertaking a new book. I have thought a hundred times that if I am to leave some traces of myself in this world it would be far more by what I have written than by what I have done. Moreover, I feel far more in a state to produce a book today than I did fifteen years ago. I have therefore set myself to seeking a subject while travelling about the mountains of Sorrento. Indeed a contemporary one and one which allows me to mix facts with ideas, the philosophy of history with history itself . . ."[18]

Thus Tocqueville follows his great master Montesquieu in the *Esprit des lois:* "It is necessary to throw light on law with history and on history with law."[19] History will explain the present. The aim of the *Democracy in America* was not only an historico-sociological analysis of American institutions but even more an examination of the European democratic problem, which American society had already foreshadowed in 1831. The *Ancien Régime* is an analysis of European society from its prerevolution-ary phase until Napoleon I. Tocqueville—I am borrowing a few sentences from the preface of our edition of this work—demon-states how the modern state creates instinctively centralization by the example of French history, and this occurs side by side with the inevitable democratization of society. However, there are two sorts of democracy, as Montesquieu already taught: free and non-free. We must determine political methods to guarantee the former.

We see quite clearly that the *two* works of Tocqueville are quite close to each other. Perhaps the study on the Revolution shows a greater precision in comparative sociology. In any case Tocqueville spared no effort in studying the social development of the three great European nations, France, England, and Germany, at their sources. The central problem in both books is, moreover, the same. "I think," Tocqueville wrote in the *Democracy in America,* "that in the democratic centuries that are beginning, individual independence and local freedom will always be the product of art. Centralisation will be the natural government."[20] And here is the passage in the *Ancien Régime* which reiterates this great lesson of French history: "The first efforts of the revolution have destroyed that great institution, monarchy, which was restored in 1800. It was not, as has been said so often, the principles of 1789 on the subject of public administration which triumphed in that time and since, but rather, on the contrary, those of the old order were all put in force again and have remained.[21]

"If I am asked how this fragment of the state of society anterior to the Revolution could thus be transplanted in its entirety and incorporated into the new state of society which has sprung up, I will answer that the principle was itself the precursor and the commencement of the Revolution; and I will add that when a people has destroyed Aristocracy in its social constitution, that people is sliding by its own weight into centralisation. Much less exertion is then required to drive it down that declivity than to hold it back. Amongst such a people all powers tend naturally to unity, and it is only by great ingenuity that they can still be kept separate."[22]

Without a doubt, Tocqueville is more certain of himself when he describes the process of centralization and its human implications in their totality than when he undertakes to discover institutional means of guaranteeing the independence of the individual. His pensive and slightly melancholy vision never led him to wish to become a political romantic; but he never ceased to ask that the new democratic, administrative and centralized system should at least accommodate the values of individuality. These values, he postulated, must be realized in a society in which rights and duties are balanced. I do not think Tocqueville went as far as one might go today. But he shows us the direction, our direction. Hic Rhodus, Hic salta! . . .

In England he found, if not the solution, at least a possible solution; and he probably was not wrong, given that this precious liberty is well protected there. Three characteristics of British political life seemed to him to make the groundwork for a conciliation between the necessities of the modern state and the imprescriptable rights of man. There was above all the coexistence of a strong central government with an efficient and vital local autonomy. Furthermore there was the role of the judiciary, with its total independence and its position above all those authorities, all of whose actions are submitted to the law. Finally, there was the fact of the openness of the English aristocracy into which everyone had the chance of rising. In spite of the fact that its younger sons formed part of the "people," they stayed linked to the aristocracy by all sorts of personal and social connections.

It is not impossible that these considerations retain their importance for us. They may require a certain transposition; and if they are capable of this, that would prove that not only Tocqueville's questions, but also his attempts to answer them, still affect us.

What Tocqueville really was aiming at was a political philosophy in which rights and duties are adequately related to one another. He fully realized that you could not have a medieval world-order, a medieval hierarchy in which everyone had his preordained place, for naturally it was evident to him that the modern class struggles have destroyed the feudal hierarchy. So the question was for him how to establish such a hierarchy on the basis of our modern world. Now this modern world has certainly established rights, more rights than we deserve. You recognize the picture of our contemporary welfare state. But the trouble with such a state is that it has only established rights and no duties. While a vague conception of duties still exists, as in my country—Great Britain—and if I knew your country better, I would venture to add the U.S.A., these traditions are vague for they are based on traditions which are no more alive and valid.

And here I see Tocqueville's great challenge—that he forces us to provide for our generation and those to come a vivid and convincing picture of how rights and duties should be perfectly balanced, implementing and holding one another; and what they explicitly mean, as explicitly as if you looked at the tables of vices and virtues of our European Gothic cathedrals. That is, ladies and gentlemen, why we have examined Tocqueville's living heritage after a hundred years—and if I may add this is why I spent on this great man so many years of my life.

BIBLIOGRAPHY AND NOTES

BIBLIOGRAPHY

In the present biographical essay in political science I have made use of the *Œuvres complètes d'Alexis de Tocqueville*, 2nd edition, Paris, 1866, published by Madame de Tocqueville. The editor is, as I have stated in the text, Gustave de Beaumont. The edition is quoted under the reference *Œuvres*, with the requisite volume noted in Roman and the page in Arabic figures.

As *primary* sources I have also used the following:

Du système pénitentiaire aux États-Unis et de son application en France, with an Appendix on the Penal Colonies and Statistical Notes, by G. de Beaumont and A. de Tocqueville, Paris, 1833.

Souvenirs de Alexis de Tocqueville, published by the Comte de Tocqueville, 2nd edition, Paris, 1893.

Correspondance entre Alexis de Tocqueville et Arthur de Gobineau, 1843–59, published by L. Schemann, Paris, 1909.

Memoir, Letters, and Remains of Alexis de Tocqueville, translated from the French by the translator of Napoleon's correspondence with King Joseph, 2 vols., London, 1861. (Quoted here under the title *Memoir.*) This edition answers to the two-volume edition of *Œuvres et Correspondance inédites d'Alexis de Tocqueville,* edited and prefaced by Gustave de Beaumont, Paris, 1861, and later embodied in the *Œuvres complètes* as vols. v and vi. To the English edition of the *Memoir* has been added de Tocqueville's article in the *London and Westminster Review,* "France before the Revolution" and his important letter to the Editor of *The Times.* (The article in the *London and Westminster Review* is to be found in French in *Œuvres,* viii, pp. 1 et seq.)

Further *primary* sources are as follows:

131

Correspondence and Conversations of Alexis de Tocqueville with Nassau William Senior, 1834–59, edited by M. C. M. Simpson, 2 vols., London, 1872.

And finally, in the series edited by myself, *Europäische Reihe: A. de Tocqueville, Autorität und Freiheit.* Schriften, Reden und Briefe ausgewählt und eingeleitet von A. Salomon, Zürich, 1935.

As *secondary* sources I have used the following (a list which does not, however, represent an exhaustive bibliography of de Tocqueville):

Bryce, James, *Studies in History and Jurisprudence,* Essay VI, London, 1901.

D'Eichthal, Eugène, *Alexis de Tocqueville et la démocratie libérale,* Paris, 1897.

Faguet, Émile, "Tocqueville" in *Politiques et moralistes du dix-neuvième siècle,* 3rd series, Paris, 1903.

Fallaux, *Madame Swetchine, sa vie et ses oeuvres,* 2 vols., Paris, 1872. Madame Swetchine, a Russian lady, was de Tocqueville's friend in his later years. She had his full confidence and he wrote to her some of his most beautiful letters. This most fascinating person, the center figure of an illustrious circle, deserves a special study which I hope to present someday to my readers.

Goering, Helmut, *Tocqueville und die Demokratie,* Munich, 1928.

Laski, Harold J., "Alexis de Tocqueville and Democracy" in *The Social and Political Ideas of some Representative Thinkers of the Victorian Age,* edited by F. J. C. Hearnshaw, London, 1933.

L'Hommedé, Edmond, *Département Français sous la monarchie de juillet. Le conseil général de la Manche et Alexis de Tocqueville. Correspondance inédite,* Paris, 1933.

Marcel, R. P., *Essai politique sur Alexis de Tocqueville,* Paris, 1910.

Mignet, M., "Alexis de Tocqueville," in *Nouveaux Éloges historiques,* Paris, 1877.

Mill, John Stuart, *Dissertations and Discussions,* vol. ii, London, 1859.

Ohaus, Werner, *Volk und Voelker im Urteil von Alexis de Tocqueville,* Berlin, 1938. This essay is a painstaking collection of the material as indicated by the title. See especially the Bibliography.

Pierson, G. W., *Tocqueville and Beaumont in America,* New York, 1938. This very comprehensive study, based on thorough research work in the family archives of the de Tocquevilles, is full of interesting material; it follows de Tocqueville's intellectual development until the publication of his work on America, obviously without the intention of interpreting his political ideas as a whole.

Redier, Antoine, *Comme disait M. de Tocqueville . . .*, Paris, 1925.

Sainte-Beuve, C. A., *Causeries du lundi*, vol. xv, Paris.

Simon, G. A., *Les Clarel à l'époque de la conquète d'Angleterre et leur descendance dans la famille Clérel de Tocqueville*, Caen, 1936.

I owe my knowledge of the existence of this last book to the kindness of Count de Tocqueville.

NOTES

CHAPTER ONE

[1] Simon, op. cit., pp. 6 et seq.

[2] Redier, op. cit., pp. 32, 33.

[3] *Œuvres*, v, pp. 15, 16.

[4] Ibid., p. 143.

[5] *Œuvres*, iii, p. 546.

[6] *Œuvres*, v, p. 151.

[7] Ibid., pp. 160, 161.

CHAPTER TWO

[1] *Œuvres*, v, p. 301. (*Memoir*, i, p. 299.)

[2] *Souvenirs*, p. 5 et seq.

[3] Redier, op. cit., pp. 85, 86.

[4] *Œuvres*, v, p. 37. (*Memoir*, i, p. 31.)

CHAPTER THREE

[1] *Œuvres*, viii, p. 327.

[2] Cf. Romano Guardini's important book on *Christliches Bewusstsein, Versuche über Pascal* (Leipzig, 1935), where, on p. 23, there is a reduced facsimile of Pascal's *Mémorial*. For its history and interpretation, ibid., pp. 25 et seq.

[3] Redier, op. cit., pp. 47 et seq.

[4] *Œuvres*, viii, p. 339.

[5] Ibid., p. 321.

[6] Ibid., pp. 321, 322.

[7] Ibid., pp. 338 et seq.

[8] *Souvenirs,* p. 122 et seq.

[9] *Œuvres,* vi, pp. 350 et seq.

[10] *Œuvres,* v, p. 429 et seq.

[11] Ibid., p. 431.

[12] Redier, op. cit., p. 125.

[13] *Œuvres,* vi, pp. 376 et seq.

CHAPTER FOUR

[1] Redier, op. cit., pp. 97 et seq.

[1a] Revising my text of 1939 I should only feel inclined to add Phillips Bradley's thoughtful introduction to the noteworthy literature on the *Democracy in America.* Cf. his edition of this work, published by Alfred A. Knopf in 1945 and since then many times reprinted. Bradley's edition is also invaluable for its rich bibliographical material. Reeve's revised translation is, however, faulty and today *entirely* inadequate. A new translation, to be published by Harper & Brothers (and by Faber & Faber, London), is in active preparation under my editorship in collaboration with Raymond Aron, Christopher Dawson, Max Lerner, David Riesman, and Fred Rodell.

[2] *Œuvres,* ii, pp. 142 et seq.

[2a] President Franklin D. Roosevelt created a new precedent. He was re-elected for a third term and in 1944 for a fourth. By the Twenty-second Amendment, ratified in 1951, the American presidency was, however, limited to two terms.

[3] *Œuvres,* v, 425 et seq.

[4] *Correspondance entre Alexis de Tocqueville et Arthur de Gobineau,* publiée par L. Schemann, p. 175.

[5] Cf. John Stuart Mill, *Dissertations and Discussions,* vol. ii, London, 1859, Essay on "M. de Tocqueville on Democracy in America," p. 3.

[6] *Œuvres,* iii, p. 485.

[7] *Ibid.,* p. 490.

[8] Ibid., p. 499.

[9] Ibid., p. 501.

[10] Ibid., p. 514.

[11] Ibid., p. 519.

[12] Ibid., p. 520 et seq.

[13] Ibid., p. 527.

[14] Ibid., p. 531.

[15] Ibid., p. 538.

[16] The MS. of this study was completed in all essentials by February 1939. George Wilson Pierson's comprehensive book *Tocqueville and Beaumont in America,* published since then (New York, 1938), has not induced me to alter anything in my own presentation.

CHAPTER FIVE

(I advise the reader to consult for this chapter the book by E. T. Gargan: *Alexis de Tocqueville: The Critical Years 1848–1851,* Washington, D.C., 1955.)

[1] *Souvenirs,* pp. 13 et seq.:

[2] *Œuvres,* vi, pp. 67, 68. (*Memoir,* ii, pp. 30, 31.)

[3] Ibid., p. 483. (Ibid., vol. ii, p. 466.)

[4] Redier, op. cit., p. 161.

[5] Ibid., p. 163.

[6] Ibid., p. 163.

[7] Ibid., p. 170.

[8] *Souvenirs,* pp. 9 et seq.

[9] Cf. Ch. Seignobos, *Histoire politique de L'Europe contemporaine: évolution des partis et des formes politiques, 1814–96,* Paris, 1908, p. 136.

[10] Arthur Rosenberg has recently given a general view of the February Revolution in France in relation to European social history since 1789 in his book *Demokratie und Sozialismus,* Amsterdam, 1938. (See also the English edition *Democracy and Socialism,* New York and London, 1939.)

[11] *Souvenirs,* pp. 102, 103.

[12] Ibid., pp. 103, 104.

[13] Ibid., p. 145.

[14] Ibid., pp. 160, 161.

[15] Ibid., pp. 276, 277.

[16] Ibid., pp. 260, 261.

[17] Ibid., p. 297.

[18] Ibid., p. 358.

[19] Ibid., p. 361.

[20] Ibid., p. 378.

[21] *Œuvres,* vii, p. 326, and *Marcel,* op. cit., pp. 408, 409.

[22] D'Eichthal, op. cit., p. 167.

[23] *Souvenirs,* pp. 313 et seq.

[24] Ibid., pp. 279 et seq.

[25] *Memoir,* ii, pp. 177, 178.

[26] Ibid., pp. 189 et seq.

[27] Cf. Maurice Paléologue's *Cavour,* London, 1927, pp. 41 et seq., and Helmuth Goering's *Tocqueville und die Demokratie,* pp. 201 et seq., Munich, 1928.

[28] Cf. B. Croce, *History of Europe in the Nineteenth Century,* London, 1934, p. 211.

CHAPTER SIX

[1] *Œuvres,* vii, p. 258.

[2] Ibid., p. 258.

[3] Ibid., p. 260.

[4] Ibid., p. 260.

[5] Ibid., p. 262.

[6] Ibid., p. 263.

[7] Ibid., pp. 263, 264.

[8] On the historiography of the literature of the French Revolution, cf. Lord Acton's *Lectures on the French Revolution,* appendix. The *Literature of the Revolution,* pp. 345 et seq., London, 1910. Also J. M. Thompson's *Robespierre,* vol. i, p. 15 et seq., Oxford, 1935. Also E. Fueter's *Geschichte der neueren Historiographie,* Munich, 1911. Also Crane Brinton's *A Decade of Revolution: 1789–99,* New York, 1934, especially the Bibliographical Essay, pp. 293 et seq. Brinton's book is to date the best modern presentation of the French Revolution as a whole.

[9] *Œuvres,* i, p. 309.

[10] Hedwig Hintze, German historian, in her important work, *Staatseinheit und Föderalismus im alten Frankreich und in der Revolution,* Stuttgart, 1928, gives a somewhat critical account from the research side of the administrative and institutional problems of French political development, but this does not in any way detract from the historical-philosophical viewpoint of *The Ancien Régime and the Revolution.*

[11] *Œuvres,* iv, pp. 18, 19. (*France before the Revolution,* p. 15.)

[12] Ibid., p. 116. (Ibid., p. 97.)

[13] Ibid., p. 118. (Ibid., p. 98.)

[14] Ibid., p. 119. (Ibid., pp. 99, 100.)

[15] Ibid., pp. 120, 121. (Ibid., p. 100.)

[16] Ibid., p. 172. (Ibid., pp. 143, 144.)

[17] Ibid., p. 227. (Ibid., p. 189.)

[18] Cf. H. Sée's *Französische Wirtschaftsgeschichte,* vol. ii, pp. 18, 19, Jena, 1936.

[19] *Œuvres,* iv, p. 259. (*France before the Revolution,* p. 215.)

[20] Ibid., p. 262. (Ibid., p. 218.)

[21] Ibid., p. 263. (Ibid., pp. 218, 219.)

[22] Ibid., p. 303. (Ibid., p. 251.)

[23] Ibid., p. 306. (Ibid., p. 253.)

[24] Ibid., p. 307. (Ibid., p. 253.)

[25] Ibid., p. 307. (Ibid., p. 254.)

[26] Ibid., p. 308. (Ibid., p. 255.)

[27] *Œuvres,* viii, pp. 170 et seq.

[28] *Œuvres,* v, pp. 460, 461.

[29] *Souvenirs,* p. 95 et seq.

[30] Cf. *Der achtzehnte Brumaire des Louis Bonaparte von Karl Marx,* edited with an introduction by J. P. Mayer, p. 20 (6th edition), Berlin, 1932.

[30a] The MS. of the present study was already completed when the author came across an important confirmation of one of his basic tenets in a very revealing book by H. D. Lasswell, the American sociologist. In his *Politics: Who Gets What, When, How,* New York, 1936, the problem of the progressive leveling-down of the dominating political classes in the mass-states of the West is most excellently analyzed. The bourgeois revolution, which began in 1789 (if we may thus summarize Lasswell's argument), came to an end in 1917 through the "mythos" of the *proletarian* revolution. With the stabilization of Soviet rule in Russia, Lasswell thinks, a new type of social revolution has appeared in Europe. I take the liberty of quoting the relevant sentences from Lasswell's book. "It may be that the common factor in the seeming political confusion of our time is the rise to power of the middle-income skill-group. Despite the contradictions and the aberrations of Russian Communism, Italian Fascism, and German National Socialism, a new world revolution may be on the march which will be realized independently of the inclusion of the world within the Soviet Union. In the name of the 'nation's workers,' and in the name of local patriotism, of anti-foreignism,

middle-income skill-groups are rising to power at the expense of aristocracy and plutocracy. Plainly the middle-income skill-groups have not yet found a common name, nor have they discerned the inner principle of sacrifice on which their unity depends; nor have they risen to the full comprehension of their historic destiny. In Europe their disunion has bred the politics of catastrophe. . . . Lacking self-consciousness, the small farmers, the small business men, the low-salaried intellectuals, and the skilled workers have fought one another rather than acted together. The labour movements of the nineteenth and twentieth centuries have, in many ways, intensified, rather than resolved, the contradictions within the middle-income skill-groups. Lacking an inspiring name and clear demands for national policy the middle-income skill-group has no myth of its virtues and its destiny. Despite every handicap, it might be argued that the middle-income skill-group is on the way to ultimate victory.

"Plainly the Italian and German movements are incidents in the process by which the last world-revolutionary pattern is both restricted and universalized. The combination of Moscow is decisively rejected; but it would be a mistake to suppose that revolution itself is dead. Restriction has proceeded by taking over some of the symbols and practices of the new pattern, even as the French revolutionary pattern spread after the emphatic rejection of the authority of the French to administer the revolution. This treatment of the Russian Revolution as the 'Second Bourgeois Revolution' may foster the march to power of middle-income skill-groups on other countries though not under the command of Moscow." This illusionless account of revolutionary processes active today in the Western social body is powerfully supported by Hermann Rauschning's recently published book, *Die Revolution des Nihilismus,* Zurich, 1938 (an abbreviated English edition has been published under the title *Germany's Revolution of Destruction,* London, 1939), in which the destructive character of the National Socialist movement, its disintegrating effect on organic social hierarchies, its "doctrineless" nature, are brilliantly and persuasively described. But the future fate of Western states and societies is not finally decided as yet, and it is still possible that opposition will arise in the deeper strata of the Western nations (England, France, and America) which will stem the threatening tide of Nihilism once again. Cf. on this subject my books *Nietzsche: Kritik und Zukunft der Kultur,* Zurich, 1935; and *Political Thought: The European Tradition,* London and New York, 1939.

[31] Redier, op. cit., pp. 229, 230.

[32] Ibid., pp. 233, 234.

[33] Ibid., p. 238.

[34] *Œuvres,* iv, p. 10. (*France before the Revolution,* p. 19.)

[35] Ibid., p. 12. (Ibid., p. 21.)

[36] Ibid., pp. 12, 13. (Ibid., p. 22.)

[37] Ibid., p. 14. (Ibid., pp. 22, 23.)

CHAPTER SEVEN

[1] *Œuvres,* v, p. 326.

[2] *Œuvres,* ix, pp. 117 et seq.

[3] Ibid., pp. 119, 120.

[4] Ibid., p. 123.

[5] *Œuvres,* vi, p. 307.

[6] Ibid., p. 439.

[7] Cf. Faguet, op. cit., pp. 73, 74, and *Souvenirs,* pp. 88 et seq.

[8] *Œuvres,* vii, p. 476.

[9] *Œuvres,* v, p. 325 et seq.

[10] Ibid., p. 447.

[11] *Œuvres,* vii, p. 500.

[12] Cf. *Correspondance entre Alexis de Tocqueville et Arthur de Gobineau,* p. 191 et seq., ed. Schemann, Paris, 1909.

[13] *Œuvres,* iv, p. 247 et seq. (*France before the Revolution,* pp. 204–6.)

[14] *Œuvres,* v, p. 395.

[15] *Œuvres,* vi, p. 231.

[16] *Souvenirs,* p. 111.

CHAPTER EIGHT

[1] *Œuvres,* vi, pp. 347, 348.

[2] Ibid., pp. 126 et seq.

[3] *Œuvres,* vii, p. 130.

[4] *Œuvres,* iii, pp. 242, 243.

[5] Redier, op. cit., p. 282.

[6] Ibid., pp. 283, 287.

[7] Ibid., p. 296.

CHAPTER NINE

[1] Cf. Paul Janet's "Alexis de Tocqueville et la science politique au XIXe siècle." *Revue des Deux Mondes,* XXXI année, Seconde Période, tome 34, pp. 110 et seq., Paris, 1861.

[2] Cf. Marx, *Poverty of Philosophy,* London, Martin Lawrence edition, pp. 101 et seq.

[3] Cf. Sorel, *Les Illusions du progrès,* Paris, 1927, p. 258.

[4] Laski, op. cit., pp. 108, 112.

[5] Cf. Dunning, *A History of Political Theories from Rousseau to Spencer,* New York, 1836, pp. 268 et seq.

[6] Cf. R. von Mohl, *Die Geschichte und Literatur der Staatswissenschaften,* Erlangen, 1855, vol. i, p. 251 and pp. 564 et seq. Also vol. iii, Erlangen, 1858, p. 94.

[7] Cf. J. C. Bluntschli's *Geschichte und Literatur des allgemeinen Staatsrechts und der Politik seit dem sechzehnten Jahrhundert bis zur Gegenwart,* Munich, 1864, p. 623.

[8] Cf. Karl Hillebrand's *Geschichte Frankreichs von der Thronbesteigung Louis Philipps bis zum Fall Napoleon III,* vol. ii, *Die Blütezeit der parlamentarischen Monarchie 1837–48,* Gotha, 1879, pp. 52 et seq.

[9] G. de Ruggiero's *History of European Liberalism,* Oxford, 1927, pp. 187 et seq.

[10] On Royer-Collard, see Laski's brilliant analysis, *Authority in the Modern State,* New Haven, 1919, pp. 281 et seq.; also Faguet, *Royer-Collard* in *Politiques et moralistes du dix-neuvième siècle,* première série, Paris, pp. 257 et seq. Royer-Collard's philosophical writings have been published by André Schimberg: *Les Fragments philosophiques de Royer-Collard,* Paris, 1913. The classical standard work on this still-too-little-known political scientist is de Barante's study *La Vie politique de M. Royer-Collard,* 2 vols., Paris, 1861. For a more recent book see *Royer-Collard: son essai d'un système politique* by Gabriel Rémond, Paris, 1933 (with a valuable bibliography).

[10a] Cf. now my book: *Max Weber and German Politics: A Study in Political Sociology,* London: Faber and Faber, 1955.

[11] Frau Marianne Weber has been so kind as to give me the following answer to my inquiry as to whether Max Weber was influenced by de Tocqueville's work: "There seems to me to be no doubt that Max Weber knew de Tocqueville's writings although I

have no actual proof of it. . . . The relationship between the historical-sociological views of the two thinkers seems to me a very credible proposition."

[12] Cf. Max Weber's *Zur Lage der bürgerlichen Demokratie in Russland*, Archives of Social Science and Social Politics, Tübingen, 1906, vol. xxii, p. 347.

[13] *Œuvres*, vi, pp. 53 et seq.

APPENDIX

[1] Cf. Sainte-Beuve, *Œuvres*, I, Pléiade edition, p. 577.

[2] Cf. J. P. Mayer, *Alexis de Tocqueville*, Paris, 1948, p. 157.

[3] Tocqueville, *Œuvres complètes*, I, 2 (ed. Mayer), p. 381.

[4] John Stuart Mill, *Dissertations and Discussions*, vol. ii, London, 1875, p. 3.

[5] Tocqueville, *Œuvres complètes*, II, 2 (ed. Mayer), p. 320.

[6] Ibid., p. 324.

[7] *Jacob Burckhardt's Briefe an seinem Freund Friedrich von Preen*, Stuttgart, 1922, p. 51.

[8] Ibid., p. 130.

[9] Tocqueville, *Œuvres complètes*, II, 1 (ed. Mayer).

[10] Marx, *Eighteenth Brumaire*, London, 1936, pp. 27 et seq.

[11] Tocqueville, *Recollections* (ed. Mayer), p. 64.

[12] Ibid., pp. 80 et seq.

[13] Tocqueville, *Œuvres complètes*, I, 2 (ed. Mayer), p. 312.

[14] Ibid., p. 313.

[15] Ibid., p. 324.

[16] Cf. Hans Freyer, *Theorie des gegenwaertigen Zeitalters*, Stuttgart, 1955, pp. 161 et seq., 169, 172. Cf. also my essay "Homme et Société" in *Critique*, Paris, 1956.

[17] Cf. my essay "Tocqueville as Political Sociologist" in *Political Studies*, vol. i, No. 2, Oxford, 1953.

[18] Ibid.

[19] Montesquieu, *De l'esprit des lois*, XXXI, 2.

[20] Tocqueville, *Œuvres complètes* (ed. Mayer), I, 2, p. 303.

[21] Ibid., p. 129.

[22] Ibid.

INDEX

Acton, Lord, 76, 109, 120, 125
Administration, communal. *See* Decentralization
Alliance, French-English, 54f.
Ampère, Jean Jacques, 120
Aristocracy, function of, 12ff., 30, 35, 37, 43, 72f., 74, 115, 127
Aristotle, 11, 18, 24, 32, 60, 89, 90

Bagehot, Walter, 60
Barnave, 76
Barthélemy, 125
Barrot, Odilon-, 56
Barrot, 51
Beaumont, Gustave de, 3, 4, 6, 9, 10, 11, 16, 21, 32, 40, 45, 53, 60, 120, 126
Beccaria, 90
Béchard, 124
Bismarck, 60, 61, 65
Blanc, Louis, 48, 68, 82
Bluntschli, J. C., 109f.
Bodin, 5, 18, 32
Bonapartism. *See* Louis Napoleon
Bossuet, 107
Bourbons, 8, 86
Bourgeoisie, English, 115f.
———, French, 7f., 43f., 72f., 74, 80f., 115
Broglie, de, 53, 125
Bryce, James, 24, 27ff., 30
Burckhardt, Jacob, 44, 60, 76, 113, 120, 125
Burke, Edmund, 11, 109, 111f., 115

Caesarism, 31. *See also* Dictatorship
Carlyle, Thomas, 67
Caussidière, 82
Cavaignac, General, 48, 52
Cavour, 63ff.
Centralization, 14f., 25, 35ff., 69ff., 113, 127
Ceti medi, 82
Chabrol, de, 2, 22
Chamberlain, H. S., 94
Chambord, Count de, 83, 84

Charles X, 2, 58
Charte of 1814, 113
Chateaubriand, 21, 117
Chéruel, 124
Church and State, 15f., 99ff., 101ff.
Cicero, 90
Civil service, 28f., 35, 114
Clérel. *See* Tocqueville, Alexis de
Comte, Auguste, 12
Constitution, American, 28f.
Corcelle, de, 53, 100
Coulanges, Fustel de, 126
Croce, 64

Danton, 82
Daumier, 81
Decentralization, 14f., 26, 37f., 40, 105
D'Eichthal, Eugène, 24, 106
Democracy, Democratization, 12, 13, 18f., 25f., 29ff., 33ff., 43f., 85f., 95, 105f., 107f., 110f., 113f., 118. *See also* Equality, Freedom, Justice
Debinski, 54
Descartes, 3, 101
Despotism. *See* Dictatorship, plebiscitary, *and* Totalitarianism
Dictatorship, plebiscitary, 37, 84. *See also* Totalitarianism
Dilthey, Wilhelm, 125
Dunning, 109

Elite, 38, 115ff.
Engels, Friedrich, 42, 53, 106
Equality, 15, 26, 27, 34ff., 41f., 75, 85, 94, 107, 113

Faguet, Émile, 91, 106
Fascism, 37, 60, 82
Flaubert, Gustave, 81
Florence, 49f.
Frantz, Constantin, 60
Freedom, 13, 15, 18f., 25, 27f., 34ff., 43, 56, 62, 63, 71, 75, 84, 85, 86, 91, 95ff., 99ff., 107, 114, 128
Freyer, Hans, 125

142